soft furnishing workbooks

simple beds

soft furnishing workbooks

simple beds

Katrin Cargill

photography by **James Merrell**

RYLAND
PETERS
& SMALL

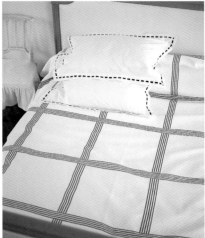

First published in Great Britain in 1998

by Ryland Peters & Small

Cavendish House

51–55 Mortimer Street

London W1N 7TD

Text © Katrin Cargill 1998

Design and photographs © Ryland
Peters & Small 1998

Produced by Sun Fung Offset
Binding Co., Ltd

Printed in China

Creative Director **Jacqui Small**

Editorial Director **Anne Ryland**

Designer **Sally Powell**

Design Assistants **Liz Brown**

Louise Cox

Megan Smith

Project Editors **Annabel Morgan**

Sophie Pearse

Editorial Assistant **Toria Leitch**

Production **Kate Mackillop**

Illustrator **Lizzie Sanders**

ISBN 1 900518 35 X

A catalogue record for this book is available from
the British Library

contents

considering we spend a large portion of our lives in bed, we owe it to ourselves to make our beds and bedrooms as comfortable and relaxing as we can. In the course of working on this book, I have seen a lot of bedrooms, some of them calm havens for relaxation and romance and others welcoming spaces conducive to unwinding from the stresses of everyday life. However, all too often the bedroom is simply a basic space for sleep, its only adornment a rumpled duvet unceremoniously thrown over the bed. Whatever happened to the slightly self-indulgent luxury of slipping between cool cotton sheets beneath a cosy woollen blanket, curling up under a snug quilt for an afternoon nap or sipping an early-morning cup of tea propped up against a comfortable padded headboard?

If we are relaxed and well rested, the trials and tribulations of life are much easier to face, and it is with this in mind that I have sought out a multitude of beautiful and inspirational ideas guaranteed to transform our places of sleep into havens of rest. A shaped upholstered headboard in a favourite fabric can change a bed from the ordinary to the unique, while a flowing, elegant bed canopy will convert an ordinary divan into a luxurious retreat. This book contains twenty inspirational and achievable projects, each one accompanied with clear and easy-to-follow step-by-step instructions. I hope it will encourage you to turn your own bedroom into a more comfortable, inviting and stylish space.

Katrin Cargill

above left Checks and stripes in combination are unified by the use of a blue and white colour scheme throughout.
left Delicate white thread embroidery enlivens the edges of a crisp cotton sheet and matching pillowcase.
below left Using ties as a fastening is a simple solution to closing covers and cases as well as an attractive decorative addition. Either make them in a contrasting fabric or use the same material for a more subtle form of embellishment.

top right The simple geometric designs of the decorative stitching on these pillowcases perfectly complements the colours and shapes of the patchwork bedspread.
above right A hot pink flanged border adds a bold and colourful note to an otherwise plain pair of white pillowcases.
below right The regimented stripes and precisely squared ends of this plump bolster are the perfect match for the bed-spread beneath, giving the bed an air of tailored elegance.

above Quilted fabric with an unusual textural quality adds interest to a pillow and creates a cosy comfortable feel.
left Linen pillowcases and sheets are the ultimate luxury. This linen pillowcase is held closed by floppy linen bows; a soft, informal look perfect for a bedroom.

pillows and sheets   A bedroom is

a place for sleep, but it is also a room where you can be a little self indulgent with your forms of decoration. Don't just stick to the usual plain bed dressings, but instead use checks or stripes to add a simple yet eye-catching area of interest. If this seems too adventurous, introduce more subtle decorative touches, such as an embroidered or contrasting border running around the edges of sheets, or ties and buttoning on pillows.

above left Lacy delicate cutwork on starched white cotton is a bed linen classic. Here a pretty daisy pattern adorns the border of a large square pillowcase.
above right An impromptu bolster case is constructed from a piece of white cotton loosely tied with a peach satin ribbon.
left A dainty drawn threadwork border embellishes these matching pillowcases. The crisp cool cotton of the bed linen is teamed with a vivid red bedspread for a cosy countrified effect.

9

buttoned bolster

This chic and stylish yet invitingly plump bolster case is made from
a colourful striped raw silk. The mouthwatering sorbet shades of the
stripes and the excess material bunched at either end of the bolster
make it reminiscent of an enormous sweet. Covering the buttons in the
same fabric and matching the colour of each button to a stripe is well
worth the effort, as this adds to the overall effect of glossy elegance.
The bolster case can be secured either with a buttoned tab or a tie.

materials & equipment

bolster pad

silk striped fabric

approximately 18 coverable buttons

instructions under flap ➤

5 Turn the fabric over so it is right side up and slit along the basting stitches. Neaten and secure the edges with buttonhole stitch. Place the fabric right side down and position the bolster in the centre. Button up the cover, making sure that there is an equal amount of fabric hanging loose at each end.

6 For a buttoned tab, cut two strips of fabric, each 8 x 14 cm (3 x 5½ in). Lay them flat and press a 5 mm (¼ in) hem around the edges to the wrong side. Fold each strip in half lengthways, wrong sides together, and neatly slip stitch the three edges closed.

7 Stitch two matching buttons to one end of the tab. Wind it round the fabric at the end of the bolster and mark two buttonholes on the fabric directly over the buttons. Slit the buttonholes and secure the raw edges with buttonhole stitch. Wrap the tie around the fabric at the ends of the bolster and fasten the buttons. The bolster pad is now held snugly within the cover.

8 Alternatively, take two strips of fabric, each 8 x 38 cm (3 x 15 in). Lay them flat and press in a 5 mm (¼ in) hem all around the edges to the wrong side. Fold the strip in half along the length, wrong sides together. Machine or slip stitch around the three open sides to complete the tie. Bunch the fabric at both ends of the bolster and secure the bolster pad by tying the strips into bows.

1 Measure the length and circumference of the bolster pad to estimate fabric quantities. The fabric must be 115 cm (45 in) longer than the bolster and 30 cm (12 in) wider than the circumference measurement. Press in a double 5 cm (2 in) hem along one long edge of the fabric. Machine stitch in place. Along the other long edge, press in a 5 cm (2 in) double hem. Slip stitch this hem in place.

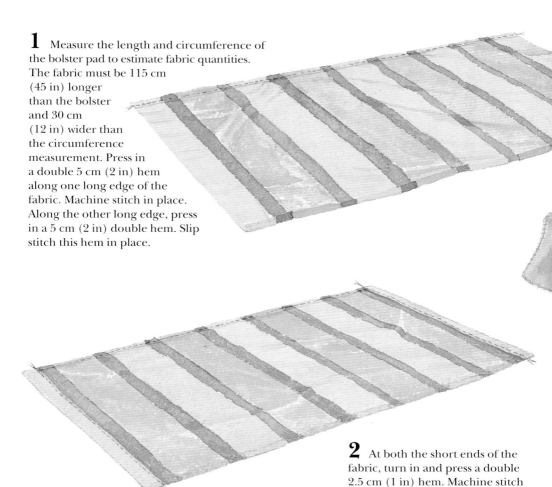

2 At both the short ends of the fabric, turn in and press a double 2.5 cm (1 in) hem. Machine stitch the hem in place, close to the inner folded edge.

3 Lay the fabric out flat, right side up. Along the machine-stitched long edge, mark positions for the buttons about 10 cm (4 in) apart and 10 cm (4 in) from the edge. Cover the buttons in the silk fabric, matching the colour of each button to the colour of a stripe. Sew each button over its matching stripe.

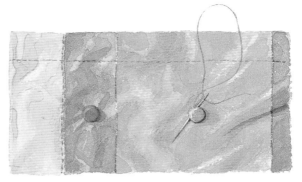

4 Turn over the fabric and place it wrong side up. Position the bolster in the centre of the fabric and wrap the fabric around it. Mark the position of each buttonhole on the fabric directly above the corresponding button. Remove the bolster and sew over the mark with small basting stitches. Make sure that the marked buttonholes are the correct size for the diameter of the buttons.

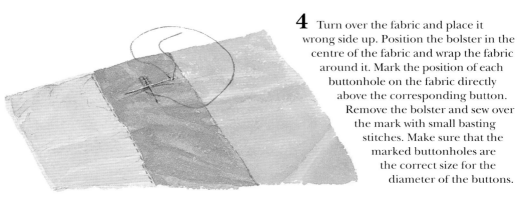

trimmed ticking

These practical and hardwearing cotton ticking pillowcases have been enlivened by the addition of jazzy red binding tape. A classic rectangular pillowcase is decorated with broad parallel stripes, while a square 'Oxford' case has a flanged, trimmed border. Unusual trimmings will make an ordinary pillowcase unique, so why not really go to town and experiment with boldly patterned braid, broad velvet ribbon, shaggy fringing or even a tactile bobbly trim.

materials & equipment

cotton ticking fabric

binding tape in a contrasting colour

instructions under flap ➤

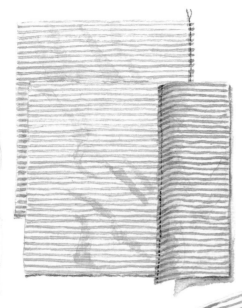

For the square flanged pillowcase

1 Measure the pillow. For the front panel, add 20 cm (8 in) to the length and 44 cm (17½ in) to the width. The stripes must run along the width. For the back panel, add 20 cm (8 in) to the length and 14 cm (5½ in) to the width. Cut out both panels.

2 On both panels, press in a 2 cm (¾ in) double hem along one side of the width. Then make a 21 cm (8¼ in) fold to the wrong side along the hemmed edge of the front panel. This flap will hold the pillow in the case.

3 Discounting the flap, mark a square on the front panel, 10 cm (4 in) from the three outer edges and 9 cm (3½ in) from the fold of the flap. Pin the binding along the inside of the marked line. At each corner, make a 90° turn and continue down the next side, tucking in the binding at the corners to form a mitre. Press the ends of the binding in at 45° to hide the raw edges. Machine stitch the binding in place.

4 Place the back panel on the front panel, right sides together. Bring 20 cm (8 in) of the flap up and over the hemmed edge of the back panel to lie on top. Pin, baste and machine stitch the side and bottom edges of the pillowcase using a 1 cm (½ in) seam allowance.

5 Snip the corners and turn the pillow right side out.

6 Working on the top of the pillow, machine stitch a seam around the outside of the red binding through all the layers of fabric. This will give the pillow a 9 cm (3½ in) wide flanged border. Make sure that you do not inadvertently sew along the top edge of the back panel, or the mouth of the pillowcase will be closed.

16

For the rectangular pillowcase

1 To calculate fabric quantities, measure the pillow (see Techniques, page 99). The front and back panels must be the same size as the pillow plus 1.5 cm (⅝ in) seam allowance all round. Add 20 cm (8 in) to the front panel. Cut out the fabric, making sure that the stripes run vertically.

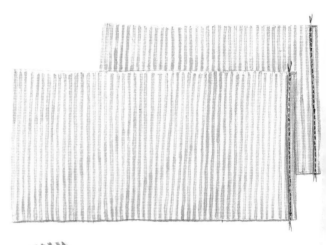

2 Press in a double 1.5 cm (⅝ in) hem along one short edge of the front and back panels.

3 On the front panel, press in a 20 cm (8 in) fold at the hemmed edge. This fold will form the pocket flap that holds the pillow snugly in the case.

4 Turn the front panel right side up. Discounting the flap, pin, baste and machine stitch two strips of red binding tape down the panel, equally spaced from the sides of the panel and each other. Snip off any excess binding.

5 Place the back panel on top of the front panel, right sides together and all raw edges aligned. Now bring the flap up and over the hemmed edge of the back panel so it lies on top.

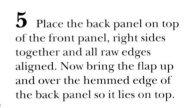

6 Pin, baste and machine stitch the two long edges and raw short edge of the pillowcase using a 1.5 cm (⅝ in) seam allowance. Reinforce the sides of the flap by machining a second seam on top of the first. Turn the pillowcase right side out and insert the pillow.

piqué pillows with bows

These invitingly plump brown gingham pillowcases are extremely easy to make, especially if you use extra-wide sheeting fabric, as you will only need a single piece of fabric that is twice the width of the pillow. The piqué panels, held in place with matching gingham bows, lend the pillowcases a demure air of modesty and old-fashioned charm.

materials & equipment

cotton gingham fabric

cotton piqué fabric

instructions under flap ➤

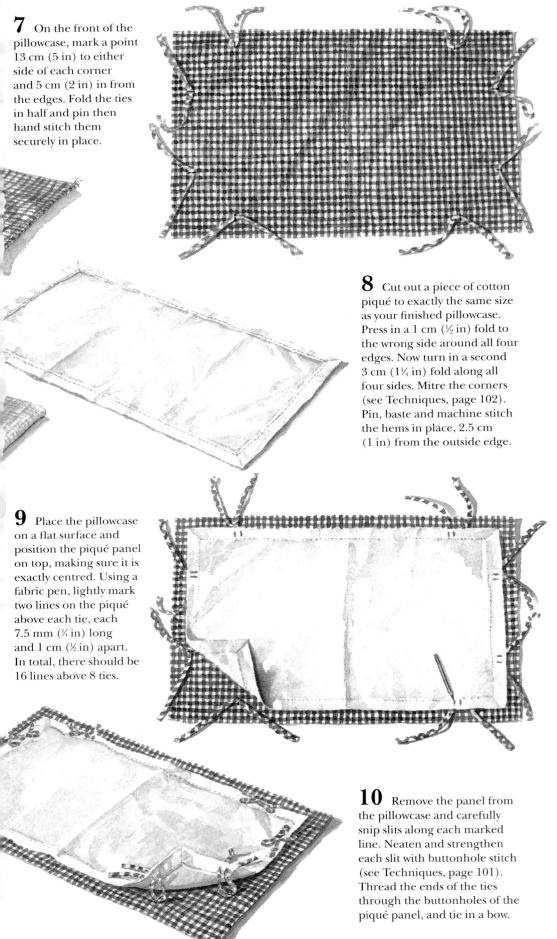

7 On the front of the pillowcase, mark a point 13 cm (5 in) to either side of each corner and 5 cm (2 in) in from the edges. Fold the ties in half and pin then hand stitch them securely in place.

8 Cut out a piece of cotton piqué to exactly the same size as your finished pillowcase. Press in a 1 cm (½ in) fold to the wrong side around all four edges. Now turn in a second 3 cm (1¼ in) fold along all four sides. Mitre the corners (see Techniques, page 102). Pin, baste and machine stitch the hems in place, 2.5 cm (1 in) from the outside edge.

9 Place the pillowcase on a flat surface and position the piqué panel on top, making sure it is exactly centred. Using a fabric pen, lightly mark two lines on the piqué above each tie, each 7.5 mm (¼ in) long and 1 cm (½ in) apart. In total, there should be 16 lines above 8 ties.

10 Remove the panel from the pillowcase and carefully snip slits along each marked line. Neaten and strengthen each slit with buttonhole stitch (see Techniques, page 101). Thread the ends of the ties through the buttonholes of the piqué panel, and tie in a bow.

1 To calculate fabric quantities, measure the width and length of your pillow (see Techniques, page 99). The fabric must be twice the width of the pillow plus an additional 26 cm (10½ in) for the flap and the seam allowances, and the same length as the pillow plus 3 cm (1¼ in) seam allowance. Cut out the fabric (see Techniques, page 100).

2 Place the fabric on a flat surface, right side up. Along the short edges of the fabric, press in a double 1.5 cm (⅝ in) hem to the wrong side. Pin, baste and machine stitch both the hems in place. Measure 20 cm (8 in) in from one hemmed end and press a fold to the wrong side of the fabric. This fold will form the pocket flap that holds the pillow snugly in the case.

3 Fold the fabric in half across the width with right sides together. The hemmed short end must be on top, and the end with the pressed flap underneath. Line up the hemmed edge of the fabric with the pressed fold of the flap. Now bring the flap up and over so it covers the hemmed edge and lies on top of the folded pillowcase.

4 Pin, baste and machine stitch all the way along the long sides of the pillowcase, stitching 1.5 cm (⅝ in) from the raw edges. Reinforce and strengthen the sides of the pocket flap by stitching a second seam on top of the first one.

5 Trim any excess fabric from each corner and, using zigzag stitch, machine stitch around the raw edges of the fabric to prevent them from fraying. Turn the pillowcase right side out.

6 Each pillowcase has eight ties. Cut eight strips of gingham, each measuring 2.5 x 32 cm (1 x 13 in), and make the ties (see Techniques, page 103). Cut the gingham strips on the bias – the ties will look decorative and have more 'give'.

velvet-edged pillowcase

A casual striped-cotton pillowcase with unexpected decorative elements – a vibrant velvet ribbon trim that emphasizes a flanged border cut from the same fabric but with a contrasting horizontal stripe. Paired with similarly trimmed white bed linen, this smart pillowcase will add a touch of style to the simplest bedroom.

materials & equipment

striped Indian cotton

2 cm (¾ in) wide velvet ribbon

instructions under flap ➤

7 Measure around the border. Cut a length of ribbon to this measurement. Pin and baste it round the outside edge of the border, overhanging the edge by 1 cm (½ in). Fold the ribbon to the other side of the border. Pin, baste and machine stitch in place, securing the ribbon on both sides of the border.

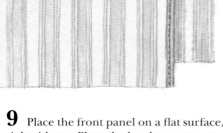

8 Take the front, back and flap panels. Press in a double 2 cm (¾ in) hem to the wrong side along one vertical edge of the back and flap panels.

9 Place the front panel on a flat surface, right side up. Place the border on top, raw inside edges aligned with the raw edges of the front panel. Pin and baste the border to the front panel all around the edges.

10 Place the back panel on top of the front panel, right side down, sandwiching the border in between the two and aligning all raw edges.

11 Take the flap and place it on top of the back panel, right side up, hemmed edge in the centre of the back panel. Pin and baste all the layers together, leaving the hemmed edge of the back panel free.

12 Machine stitch all around the pillowcase using a 1.5 cm (⅝ in) seam allowance. Do not stitch up the hemmed end of the back panel.

13 Turn the pillowcase right side out and insert the pillow.

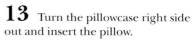
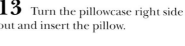

1 To estimate fabric quantities, measure the pillow (see Techniques, page 99). Cut out front and back panels that are both the same size as the pillow plus an extra 1.5 cm (⅝in) seam allowance all round. For the flap that holds the pillow in the case, cut a piece of fabric 30 cm (12 in) wide and the same length as the pillow, with a 1.5 cm (⅝in) seam allowance all round.

2 For the border, cut out four strips of fabric, each 22 cm deep, (8½ in) two to the width of the pillow plus 18 cm (7 in) and two to the length of the pillow plus 18 cm (7 in).

3 Take the strips of fabric and fold each one in half widthways, wrong sides together. Press the strips to mark a central fold line.

4 Open out each strip and place it on a flat surface, right side down. Fold the ends into a mitre and press. Cut along the fold lines to create triangular points at the ends of the strips.

5 Place the strips corner to corner, right sides together, alternating a long strip with a short strip. Pin, baste and stitch the strips together at their triangular ends, using a 1 cm (½ in) seam allowance.

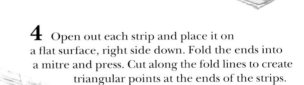

6 Turn the attached strips right side out and press the completed border along the fold line to form a large rectangular frame.

red-trimmed linen

Cool linen sheets and pillowcases are irresistibly inviting after a long day. Here, square pillows have been encased in linen pillowcases trimmed with boldly coloured faggotting for a cosy, countrified effect. Teamed with a matching sheet and a simple gingham bedspread, they bring a charming air of simplicity to a bedroom.

materials & equipment

white cotton or linen fabric

2 cm (¾ in) wide trim

instructions under flap ➤

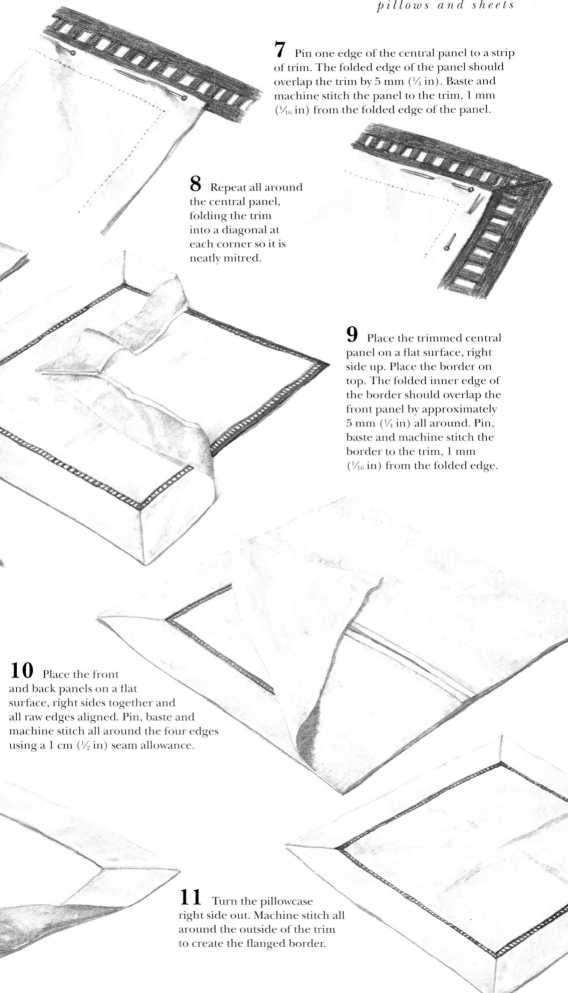

7 Pin one edge of the central panel to a strip of trim. The folded edge of the panel should overlap the trim by 5 mm (¼ in). Baste and machine stitch the panel to the trim, 1 mm (¹⁄₁₆ in) from the folded edge of the panel.

8 Repeat all around the central panel, folding the trim into a diagonal at each corner so it is neatly mitred.

9 Place the trimmed central panel on a flat surface, right side up. Place the border on top. The folded inner edge of the border should overlap the front panel by approximately 5 mm (¼ in) all around. Pin, baste and machine stitch the border to the trim, 1 mm (¹⁄₁₆ in) from the folded edge.

10 Place the front and back panels on a flat surface, right sides together and all raw edges aligned. Pin, baste and machine stitch all around the four edges using a 1 cm (½ in) seam allowance.

11 Turn the pillowcase right side out. Machine stitch all around the outside of the trim to create the flanged border.

1 The back panel is made from two pieces of fabric. Measure the pillow pad and add 20 cm (8 in) to the width and the length. Add a further 12 cm (5 in) to the width. Divide this measurement by two to calculate the size of each piece.

2 Cut out the back panels. Press in a 1 cm (½ in) single hem along one long side of each panel. Pin, baste and machine stitch in place. Place the panels on a flat surface, right sides together and hemmed edges aligned. Seam along the hemmed sides, 5 cm (2 in) in from the hemmed edge. Leave a 40 cm (16 in) opening in the centre of the seam. Open out and press the seam.

3 For the central panel, cut out a square of fabric to the size of the pillow pad plus 1 cm (½ in) seam allowance all round. Press in a 1 cm (½ in) hem around all four edges.

4 Cut out four strips of trim, each one 2 cm (¾ in) longer than the sides of the central panel minus the seam allowance.

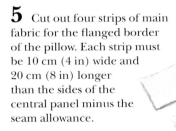

5 Cut out four strips of main fabric for the flanged border of the pillow. Each strip must be 10 cm (4 in) wide and 20 cm (8 in) longer than the sides of the central panel minus the seam allowance.

6 Place two border strips right sides together. Pin and baste the strips together at a 45° angle from the top corner. Check that the angle of the seam is correct then machine stitch, stopping 1 cm (½ in) from the bottom of the strip. Attach the other strips in the same way until the border is complete. Press open the seams then press a 1 cm (½ in) hem to the wrong side all around the inside of the border.

right A plump feather eiderdown covered in a homely check makes a snug and warm winter bedspread. The channel quilting holds the filling in place and prevents any lumping.
below Crocheted cotton bedspreads are available in a wide range of patterns and colours. This is a fine example of intricate white-on-white crochet work, topped with a cotton bolster.

bedspreads

Bedspreads have a dual function – to provide warmth and decoration. Whether your preference is for dainty florals or bold tailored stripes, your bedspread must be both attractive and inviting, and its fabric and design should suggest comfort and a hint of luxury.

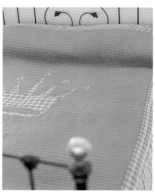

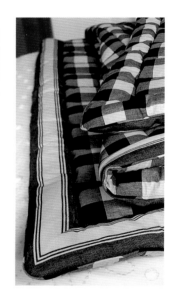

above left Graphic stripes and unusual surface texturing enhance a simple sleigh bed.
above centre A complementary coloured checked border and a matching appliquéd crown motif give an old wool blanket a new lease of life.
above right A bold black and ecru checked eiderdown creates a cosy yet contemporary effect.
left A floral cotton sheet with ruffled border makes a pretty summer bedspread.

top left Quilted blue and white checks are smartly teamed with toning ticking.
top centre A crisp white cotton bedspread made from Marseilles cloth. Jacquard would create a similar effect.
top right A faded country quilt to snuggle up beneath.
left This colourful bedspread is cleverly constructed from remnants of antique ticking.
below A fine wool blanket embellished with decorative embroidery and a loopy trim.
bottom left Delicate lace work has an air of distinction.
bottom right An antique floral eiderdown with a beguiling air of old-fashioned charm.

appliquéd quilted bedspread

This bedspread is made from matelasse, a thick double cloth with a quilted effect. A crisp blue-striped ribbon has been appliquéd to the bedspread in a bold and geometric pattern of squares. It is essential that the bedspread itself is an exact square, so no unevenly sized squares or crooked lines can mar its perfection.

materials & equipment

220 x 220 cm (85 x 85 in) matelasse fabric

27 m (81 ft) striped ribbon

instructions under flap ➤

7 Check that the ribbons run straight and are exactly parallel to each other. Machine stitch them in place along both edges, stitching in the same direction along each side to prevent the ribbon from puckering.

8 Take another four strips of ribbon and repeat steps 5, 6 and 7, this time positioning the ribbons so their upper long edge aligns with the horizontal marked lines on the bedspread.

9 Turn in and press a 5 mm (¼ in) hem to the right side all around the edges of the bedspread.

10 There should be four strips of ribbon left to border the bedspread. At each end of the first strip, fold the ribbon diagonally to the wrong side at a 45° angle. Press in place. Repeat this procedure with the three remaining lengths of ribbon.

11 Place the first strip right side up along one edge of the bedspread over the hemmed edges of the matelasse, aligning the folded edge of the bedspread with the outside edge of the ribbon. Pin and baste in place. Repeat along the next edge of the bedspread. At the corners, the pressed diagonal edges should meet up exactly to form a mitre.

12 When the ribbon is basted in place around the four sides of the bedspread, machine stitch down both sides of the ribbon. Make sure that each seam is stitched in the same direction so that the ribbon does not pucker.

13 Slip stitch the mitred corners of the ribbon closed. Press the bedspread and place on the bed.

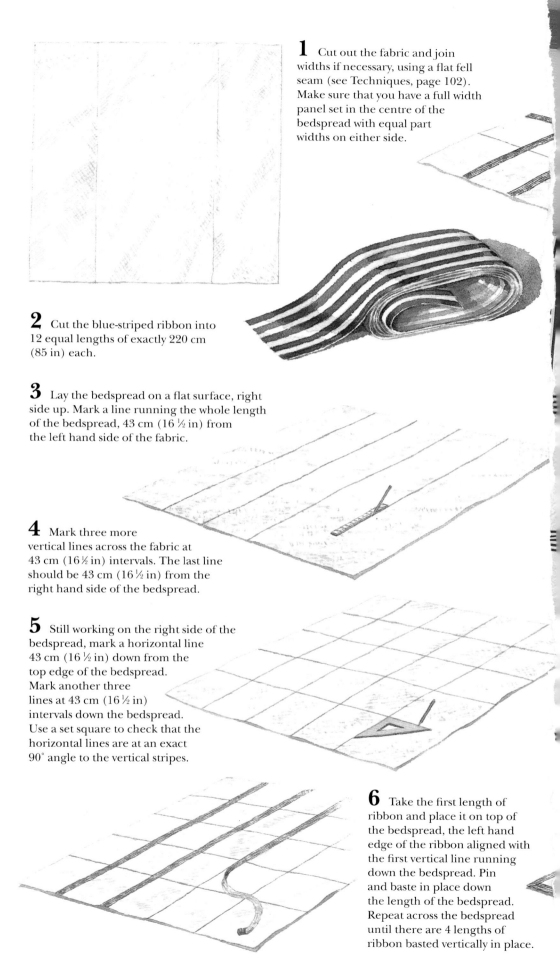

1 Cut out the fabric and join widths if necessary, using a flat fell seam (see Techniques, page 102). Make sure that you have a full width panel set in the centre of the bedspread with equal part widths on either side.

2 Cut the blue-striped ribbon into 12 equal lengths of exactly 220 cm (85 in) each.

3 Lay the bedspread on a flat surface, right side up. Mark a line running the whole length of the bedspread, 43 cm (16 ½ in) from the left hand side of the fabric.

4 Mark three more vertical lines across the fabric at 43 cm (16½ in) intervals. The last line should be 43 cm (16 ½ in) from the right hand side of the bedspread.

5 Still working on the right side of the bedspread, mark a horizontal line 43 cm (16 ½ in) down from the top edge of the bedspread. Mark another three lines at 43 cm (16 ½ in) intervals down the bedspread. Use a set square to check that the horizontal lines are at an exact 90° angle to the vertical stripes.

6 Take the first length of ribbon and place it on top of the bedspread, the left hand edge of the ribbon aligned with the first vertical line running down the bedspread. Pin and baste in place down the length of the bedspread. Repeat across the bedspread until there are 4 lengths of ribbon basted vertically in place.

featherstitched patchwork quilt

This cosy patchwork quilt, made from scraps and remnants
of antique blue and white printed cotton, is not handstitched in the
traditional way. Instead, the quilt is machine sewn to save time and
effort. Feather-stitching in a complementary colour scrambles over
and around the seams, providing a decorative finishing touch.

materials & equipment

a wide variety of scraps and remnants of fabric for the patchwork

upholstery wadding

backing fabric for the quilt

embroidery needle

silk embroidery thread

instructions under flap ➤

7 Lay the finished piece of patchwork on a flat surface, right side down. Place the wadding on top, aligning all raw edges. Pin, baste and machine stitch around the sides of the wadding, using a 1 cm (½ in) seam allowance. Run a line of stitching down and across some of the seams of the patchwork to hold the wadding in place.

8 Turn over the quilt so the patchwork is right side up. Feather stitch all over the seam lines, using silk embroidery thread (see Techniques, page 101).

9 Place the quilt right side up on a flat surface and put the backing fabric on top, right side down. Pin, baste and machine stitch around the edges, using a 1.5 cm (⅝ in) seam allowance. Leave a 50 cm (20 in) section unseamed at one end in order to turn the quilt right side out.

10 Turn the quilt right side out. Press in a 1.5 cm (⅝ in) hem to the wrong side along the unseamed section. Slip stitch the opening closed. Press the finished quilt and place it on the bed.

1 Measure up your bed (see Techniques, page 99) to calculate how much fabric you will need. The backing fabric and the finished piece of patchwork must be the size of the finished quilt plus 2 cm (¾ in) added all round. The wadding must also be the size of the finished quilt but without seam allowances.

2 Each patchwork square is 10 x 10 cm (4 x 4 in) plus an additional 1 cm (½ in) seam allowance. To work out how many squares you will need for the quilt, divide the width and the length of the finished quilt by 10 (or 4 if you are using inches). To calculate how many squares you will need in total, multiply the number of squares that will run across the quilt by the number that will run down the quilt.

3 Make a square template measuring 11 x 11 cm (4 ½ x 4 ½ in) from stiff card.

4 Amass all your scraps and remnants of fabric. Place the template on the wrong side of a scrap. Mark around it then remove it. Cut out the square. Position your template carefully to enable you to get as many squares as possible from each piece of material.

5 When you have cut out the requisite number of squares, place two squares right sides together. Pin, baste and machine stitch down one side, using a 5 mm (¼ in) seam allowance. Press the seam flat. Seam another square to one of the attached squares. Continue until you have a strip of squares to the width of your bedspread.

6 Make strips until you have enough for the length of the quilt. Place one strip on top of another, right sides together. Pin, baste and machine stitch along one long edge, using a 5 mm (¼ in) seam allowance. Press the seam flat. Continue to piece the strips together until the patchwork is the desired size.

stencilled duvet cover

The simple but effective craft of stencilling is not limited to walls and woodwork. A little imagination and a stencil kit are all that are needed to transform a plain duvet cover into something totally unique. Here, garlands of oak leaves have been stencilled on to a cotton ticking duvet cover in washable fabric paint.

materials & equipment

cotton ticking fabric

stencil-making kit

washable white, grey and black paint

stencil brush

fine brush

plain fabric for border and ties

instructions under flap ➤

7 Place the border on the front panel, right side down. Pin the inside edges of the border to the raw edges of the front panel. At the corners, fold the excess material to one side. Pin and baste the border to the front panel.

8 Machine stitch the border to the front panel, using a 1.5 cm (⅝ in) seam allowance. Do not stitch over the mitres in the corners.

9 When the border is stitched to the front panel around all the edges, press it out flat, away from the front panel.

10 Place the front and back panels right sides together, aligning all the raw edges. Pin, baste and machine stitch the panels together all around the four sides using a 1.5 cm (⅝ in) seam allowance. Leave a 50 cm (20 in) section unseamed at one end as an opening for the duvet.

11 Along the unseamed section, press in a 1.5 cm (⅝ in) hem to the wrong side. Neatly slip stitch the hem in place.

12 Cut four strips of fabric, each one 5 x 41 cm (2 x 16½ in), and make the ties (see Techniques, page 103). Hand sew the ties to the inside of the open section. Turn the duvet cover right side out, insert the duvet and knot the ties.

1 To calculate fabric quantities, measure the duvet (see Techniques, page 99). For the back panel add 6.5 cm (2½ in) to the width and the length. The front panel should be 16.5 cm (7¾ in) shorter in width and length than the back panel. Join widths as necessary (see Techniques, page 100). Cut out both panels. For the border, cut four strips of plain fabric, each 18 cm (7 in) deep, two the same length as the back panel and two equal in length to the width of the back panel. You will also need enough of the border fabric to make four ties.

2 Make a template for one leaf (see Templates, page 105). On a sheet of paper, draw a circle with a 25 cm (10 in) diameter. Draw a garland of eight leaves around the circle. Use a stencil kit to transfer the design to a stencil card and cut it out.

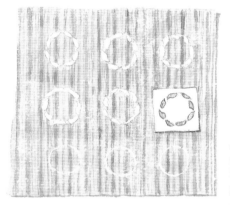

3 Place the front panel on a flat surface, right side up. Divide it into equal sections, one for each garland. Position the stencil in the central section and stencil the garland on to the fabric, using the white paint.

4 Leave the paint until it is completely dry. Then, using a fine brush, hand paint the detail on the leaves, using the grey paint.

5 Using black paint, add a shadow around the outline of the leaves. Leave the paint to dry.

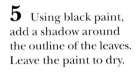

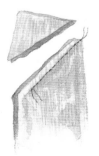

6 Place a top and a side border strip right sides together, aligning the raw edges. At one end, pin and baste the strips together at a 45° angle from the top corner. Check the angle of the seam then machine stitch, stopping 1.5 cm (⅝ in) from the bottom edge. Trim the corners. Attach the other strips in the same way to complete the border.

velvet-edged bedspread

This lightweight summer bedspread is made from a crisp striped cotton and edged with plush brown velvet piping for an effect that is both simple and sophisticated. The bedspread is only intended to fall halfway to the floor on either side, drawing attention to the rhythmic curves of the neatly piped scalloped edging.

materials & equipment

striped cotton fabric

velvet piping

instructions under flap ➤

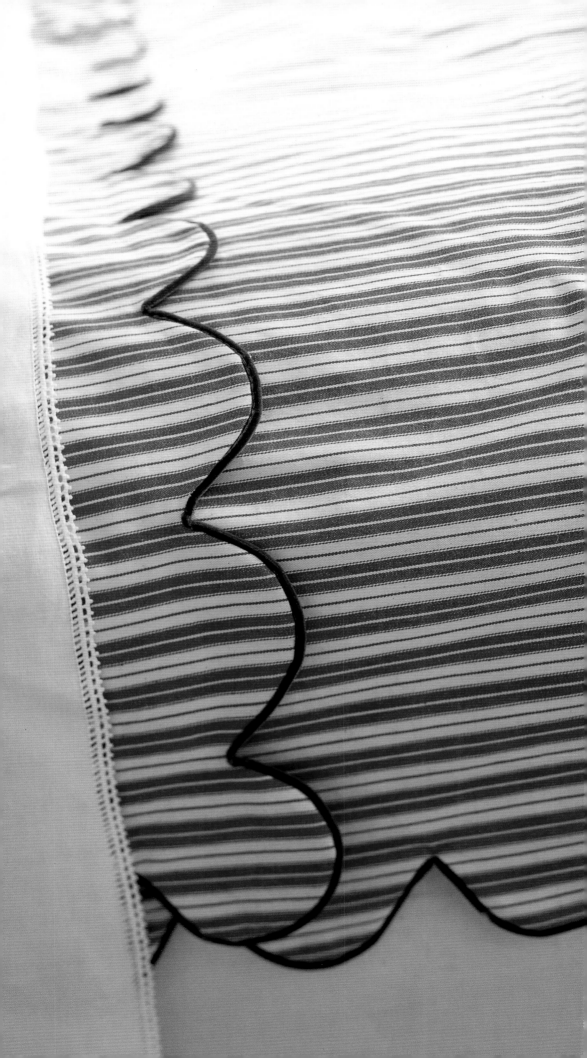

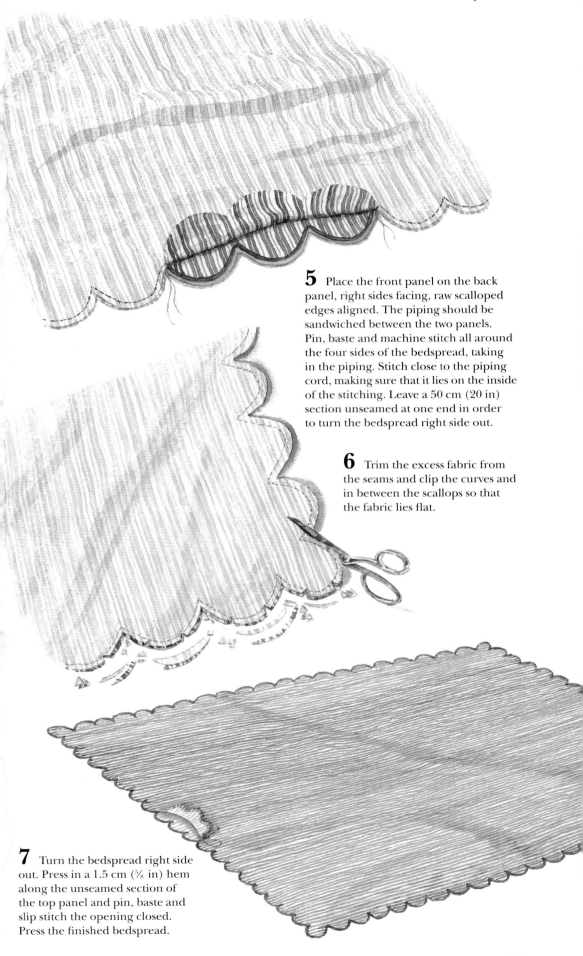

5 Place the front panel on the back panel, right sides facing, raw scalloped edges aligned. The piping should be sandwiched between the two panels. Pin, baste and machine stitch all around the four sides of the bedspread, taking in the piping. Stitch close to the piping cord, making sure that it lies on the inside of the stitching. Leave a 50 cm (20 in) section unseamed at one end in order to turn the bedspread right side out.

6 Trim the excess fabric from the seams and clip the curves and in between the scallops so that the fabric lies flat.

7 Turn the bedspread right side out. Press in a 1.5 cm (⅝ in) hem along the unseamed section of the top panel and pin, baste and slip stitch the opening closed. Press the finished bedspread.

1 Measure the bed to calculate fabric quantities (see Techniques, page 99). This bedspread is not intended to reach to the floor, so adjust your measurements accordingly. Cut out a front and back panel for the bedspread. A single bedspread may only require one width of 135 cm (54 in) fabric but for a double bedspread you will have to join widths (see Techniques, page 100).

2 When joining widths make sure that there is a full width in the centre of the bedspread with equal part widths at each side.

3 Make a template for the scalloped edges of the bedspread (see Templates, page 105). Pin the front and back panels right sides together. Place the template on the uppermost panel, positioning it right at the raw edges. Mark around the template. Continue around all four sides of the bedspread. Cut around the marked line through both thicknesses of fabric.

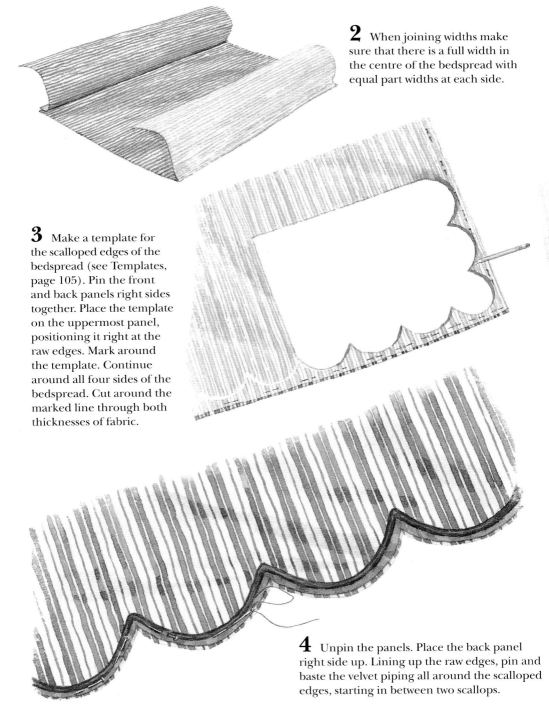

4 Unpin the panels. Place the back panel right side up. Lining up the raw edges, pin and baste the velvet piping all around the scalloped edges, starting in between two scallops.

valances

serve a practical purpose, concealing unattractive bed bases, stumpy bed legs and under-bed storage areas. Over-elaborate specimens made up in flouncy, fussy designs have earned valances a bad reputation. However, this is undeserved, for a tailored valance with inverted pleats can be extremely elegant, while a delicate lace-trimmed valance made from antique cotton sheets will add distinction to any bedroom.

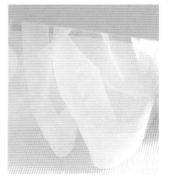

left and above Fine organza with a deep double hem billows out beneath a simple wooden-framed bed. Despite its fragile, flimsy appearance, organza is extremely strong, making it a luxurious yet practical choice for soft furnishings. *below* In a guest bedroom, a blue and white theme boldly combines checks, stripes and flowers, and demonstrates how different patterns can be harmoniously linked by colour alone. This stylish effect has been achieved on a tight budget – the valances are fashioned from humble tea towels.

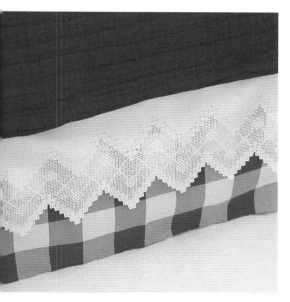

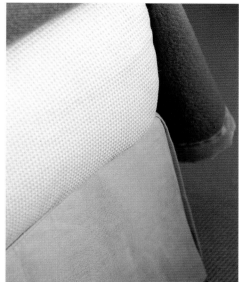

above The graphic lines and chunky red
and white blocks of this checked valance are
softened by the unexpected addition of a soft
white lace trim at the top of the valance.
below left and right A colourful red and white
checked cotton is sewn into precise box
pleats in this cheerful valance, which makes
the bed the focal point in this small bedroom.

bottom left A delicate white scalloped sheet
used as a valance hangs just above floor level,
peeping out from beneath an exquisitely
detailed quilted bedspread.
above right A simple yet sophisticated linen
valance with an inverted pleat at the corners
adds a unfussy note of comfort to a cool
contemporary interior.

tailored pictorial print

Toile de Jouy, a cotton fabric printed with idyllic pastoral scenes in muted tones, is ideally suited to a relaxed and soothing bedroom environment. If made up in frilly, fussy bed dressings, the effect can be a little too twee. However, *toile de Jouy* is ideally suited to the simple uncluttered lines of this smart, precisely pleated valance.

materials & equipment

toile de Jouy *fabric*

lining fabric

piping cord

bias binding (in the same colour as the piping cord)

instructions under flap ➤

7 Make a strip of bias binding that is equal in length to the bottom edge of the joined skirt (see Techniques, page 103). Press a 5 mm (¼ in) fold to the wrong side along both long edges, then press the strips in half so that the folded edges meet.

8 Insert the bottom raw edge of the skirt into the folded bias binding. Pin, baste and machine stitch the binding in place along both sides of the bottom edge of the skirt, close to the folded edge of the binding.

9 Mark a line 14 cm (5½ in) to each side of the pleat panels. Fold the end and side panels along these lines so they meet over the pleat sections. Pin then baste the pleats in place.

10 Make a length of piping equal to the top edge of the valance skirt.

11 Place the central panel on a flat surface and pin the piping around the sides and unhemmed end of the central panel, aligning all raw edges.

12 Place the skirt on the central panel, right side down, all raw edges aligned and the pleats positioned exactly at the corners of the main panel. The piping should be sandwiched between the two. Pin, baste and machine stitch a seam 1.5 cm (⅝ in) from the raw edges, ensuring that the piping cord is on the inside of the stitching.

13 Press the finished valance and place it on the bed base.

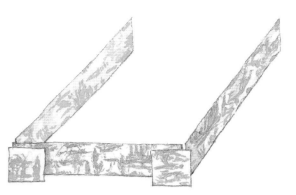

1 To calculate fabric quantities, measure the bed (see Techniques, page 99). The valance skirt is made from five pieces of fabric. Cut two side panels, the length of the bed plus 15 cm (6 in) and an end panel, equal to the width of the bed plus 30 cm (12 in). Add 1.5 cm (⅜ in) seam allowance to the length. Cut two pieces of fabric for the pleats, each 30 cm (12 in) long and the height of the side and end panels.

2 The central panel of the valance, which is concealed by the mattress, is made of lining fabric bordered with *toile de Jouy*. For the lining panel, deduct 30 cm (12 in) from the length and width of the bed base. Cut out the lining to these measurements, joining widths if necessary (see Techniques, page 100).

3 To border the lining panel, cut four strips of *toile*, two 18 cm (7 in) wide and the same length as the bed base plus 5 cm (2 in) and two 18 cm (7 in) wide and equal to the width of the bed base plus 5 cm (2 in).

4 Place a long and a short border strip right sides together, all raw edges aligned. Pin and baste the strips together at a 45° angle running diagonally down from the top corner. Check that the angle of the seam is correct then machine stitch. Stop stitching 1.5 cm (⅜ in) from the bottom edge of the strip. Attach the other strips in the same way until the border is complete. Press open the seams then press a 1.5 cm (⅜ in) fold to the wrong side all around the inside edge of the border.

5 Place the central lining panel right side up on a flat surface and lay the border over it, also right side up, making sure the edges overlap evenly all round. Pin, baste and machine stitch the border to the central panel. At the top (bedhead) end of the border, press in a double 6 mm (¼ in) hem.

6 Take the three pieces of fabric for the skirt and the two narrower pieces of fabric for the inverted pleats. With right sides together, join one side of each corner pleat to a side panel, then the other side of the corner pleat to an end panel. Pin, baste and machine stitch in place.

soft green scallops

This simple but decorative scalloped valance is designed especially for a single bed with a headboard and footboard, and is the perfect partner for the scalloped corona (see pages 82–84). However, the valance looks equally effective on its own, and is guaranteed to add an air of elegant simplicity to any bedroom. If you have an ordinary divan without a footboard, add a third section of scalloped skirt for the end of the bed.

materials & equipment

cotton fabric

lining fabric

instructions under flap ➤

6 Place the seamed valance skirt on a flat surface and fold a 1.5 cm (⅝ in) hem to the wrong side of the fabric all along the top raw edges of the lining and main fabric. Press the hem in place, making sure that the folded edges meet along the top of the skirt panel.

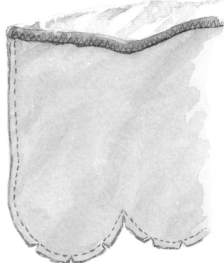

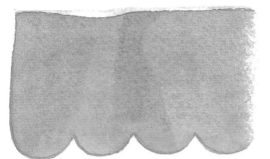

7 Turn both of the valance skirts right side out and press flat.

8 Take the piece of lining for the central panel of the valance. Place it on a flat surface and press in a 1.5 cm (⅝ in) hem all around the sides of the fabric. Pin, baste and machine stitch the hem in place.

9 Place the central lining panel on a flat surface, right side up. Insert one long edge of the lining panel in between the folded top edges of a skirt panel. Make sure that at least 2.5 cm (1 in) of the lining is sandwiched between the top edges of the skirt. Pin, baste and machine stitch the skirt to the central panel, stitching close to the folded edges of the skirt panels.

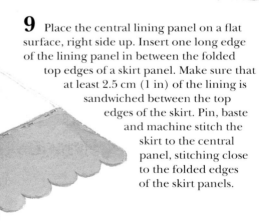

10 Position the valance on the bed base then place the mattress on the base and arrange the bed as desired.

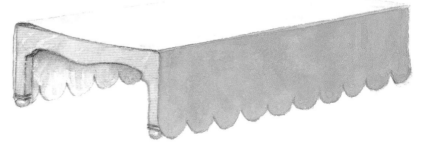

1 The central panel of the valance is made from lining fabric, while the skirt consists of two lined cotton panels with scalloped edges. To calculate fabric quantities, measure your bed (see Techniques, page 99). Add 5 cm (2 in) to the length and width of the central panel plus 1.5 cm (⅝ in) seam allowance all round. The skirt must be long enough to cover the bed base but not so long that it touches the floor. Add a 1.5 cm (⅝ in) seam allowance all round. Cut out the fabric and lining.

2 Make a template for the scalloped edge of the valance (see Templates, page 105). Pin the template to the bottom of a skirt panel and mark around the outline. Remove the template and cut along the marked line. Repeat for the other panel and the lining panels.

3 Zigzag stitch along the top raw edges of the lining and main fabric.

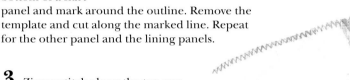

4 Place a skirt panel on a lining panel, right sides together. Pin, baste and machine stitch the two panels together all around the sides and scalloped bottom of the panels, using a 1.5 cm (⅝ in) seam allowance. Leave the top of the valance open. Attach the other skirt and lining panel in the same way.

5 Clip around the curves and in between the scallops to prevent any puckering or bulkiness.

appliquéd zigzags

This bold valance, with its zigzagged edges, strikes a note of warmth and vitality in an otherwise cool and uncluttered bedroom. The hot pink colour and solid shapes of the valance are a perfect foil for the graceful fluid outline of an antique brass bedstead. A homely checked fabric, which tones perfectly with the pink of the valance, has been used for the duvet cover and cut into diamond-shaped lozenges, which are used to appliqué the valance.

materials & equipment

plain cotton fabric

checked cotton or gingham

lining fabric

instructions under flap ➤

10 Take the checked fabric and cut out a series of squares, each 10 x 10 cm (4 x 4 in). There should be a square for every zigzag along the bottom of the valance, and a half square for the half zigzags at the corners.

11 Turn each square at an angle so that it is diamond shaped. Place one 7 cm (3 in) above the point of each zigzag. Pin and baste the diamonds in place. Overlock the raw edges of each diamond in a thread that matches the main fabric.

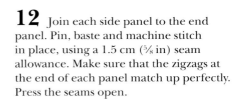

12 Join each side panel to the end panel. Pin, baste and machine stitch in place, using a 1.5 cm (⅝ in) seam allowance. Make sure that the zigzags at the end of each panel match up perfectly. Press the seams open.

13 Place the skirt on the central panel, right side down, all raw edges aligned. Match up the seams in the skirt panel to the corners of the central panel. Pin, baste and machine stitch the two together, using a 1.5 cm (⅝ in) seam allowance.

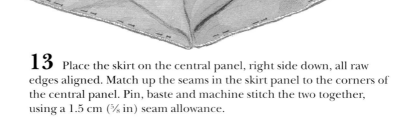

14 Press the valance and position it on the bed base.

1 To calculate fabric quantities, measure the bed (see Techniques, page 99). The skirt of the valance is made from three pieces of fabric. Cut two side panels to the length of the sides of the bed, and one end panel to the width of the end of the bed. Add a 1.5 cm (⅝ in) seam allowance to the depth of the skirt.

2 The central panel of the valance, which is concealed by the mattress, is made of lining fabric bordered with main fabric. For the lining panel, deduct 30 cm (12 in) from the length and width of the bed base. Cut out the lining fabric to these measurements. Join widths if necessary (see Techniques, page 100).

3 To border the central lining panel, cut four strips of main fabric, two of them 18 cm (7 in) wide and the same length as the sides of the bed base plus 5 cm (2 in), and the other two 18 cm (7 in) wide and the same width as the ends of the bed base plus 5 cm (2 in).

4 Place a long and a short strip right sides together. Pin and baste the strips together at a 45° angle from the top corner. Check that the angle is correct then machine stitch, stopping 1.5 cm (⅝ in) from the bottom of the strip. Attach the other strips until the border is complete. Press open the seams then press a 1.5 cm (⅝ in) fold to the wrong side all around the inside edge of the border.

5 Place the lining panel right side up with the border on top, right side up. Make sure the edges overlap evenly all round. Pin, baste and machine stitch the two together. At the top (bedhead) end, press in a double 6 mm (¼ in) hem. Pin, baste and machine stitch in place.

6 Each zigzag is 15 cm (6 in) wide. Divide the width of each finished skirt panel by 15 (6) to work out how many zigzags will run along each side of the valance. If the width is not exactly divisible by 15 (6), adjust the size of the zigzag until the width of the zigzag divides the width of each panel exactly. Make the template (see Templates, page 104).

7 Take the three pieces of fabric for the skirt and pin the two side panels right sides together.

8 Place the pinned side panels on a flat surface. Measure 1.5 cm (⅝ in) from the side of the panel (for the seam allowance) and place the template on the panels. Draw round the outline. Continue all the way across the fabric. Finish with a half zigzag and 1.5 cm (⅝ in) seam allowance. Cut along the marked line and unpin the panels. Repeat for the end panel.

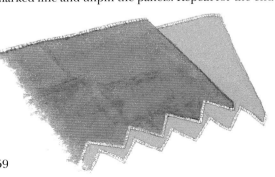

9 Using white thread, overlock the raw edges all along the top and zigzagged bottom of each panel.

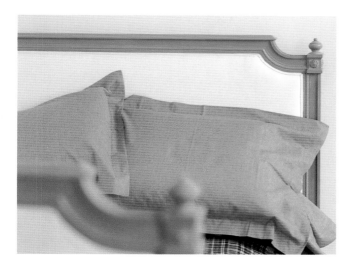

headboards

Without a headboard, a bed can have a rather forlorn, unfinished appearance, while an attractive headboard makes any bed a focal point. Upholstered headboards lend themselves to all kinds of imaginative treatments and can be matched to other soft furnishings for an integrated effect.

left Natural textures and geometric shapes combine to create a cool contemporary look in this stylish bedroom. The oversized headboard, upholstered in beige cotton and covered with a white cotton panel, provides an unobtrusive backdrop for the luxurious bed. *above left* Wooden headboards with an upholstered panel in the centre are extremely versatile – a change of fabric on the panels will completely transform the character of the bed. Here, a plain white

cotton panel draws attention to the elegant lines of the carved wooden bedframe. *above right* A plumply padded headboard is upholstered in an abstract print. Matching piping on the back and front of the headboard emphasizes the shaped corners. *below right* On a kingsize bed, the sheer size of the headboard can be overpowering, but here the effect is minimized by the use of a pretty *toile de Jouy* fabric and by shaping the sides to make the headboard appear narrower.

above A narrow red stripe creates an elegant tailored effect on a rectangular headboard. The narrow piping provides a smart yet subtle finishing touch. Crisp white cotton bed linen is the perfect partner for this stylish headboard.

florals and checks

This padded and shaped headboard is covered with a fitted
slipcover made from an 1950s-style printed fabric that combines
small checks with rose-scattered stripes. Although the headboard will
add a note of cosiness and comfort to any bedroom, it is ideally suited
to a guest bedroom, for the warm colours and the pretty fabric make it
particularly inviting. For a simpler, more formal effect, use plain fabric
and team it with boldly coloured contrasting piping and ties.

materials & equipment

2 cm (¾ in) thick plywood for the headboard

upholstery wadding

wood glue

staple gun

printed cotton fabric

lining fabric

contrasting piping

instructions under flap ➤

8 Make a length of piping cord from the main fabric and a length from contrastingly coloured fabric (see Techniques, page 103). Both pieces must be the length of the gusset strip. Place the front panel right side up on a flat surface and pin and baste the contrasting piping around the side and top edges, lining up the raw edges.

9 Cut 12 strips of main fabric, each one 4 x 50 cm (1½ x 20 in), and make 12 ties (see Techniques, page 103).

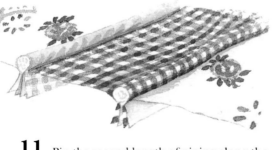

10 Pin the gusset strip to the front panel, right sides together, so the contrasting-coloured piping is in between the two pieces of fabric. Along one straight edge of the panel, slip three ties between the piping and the gusset, the first tie 20 cm (8 in) up from the bottom of the panel and the next two at 20 cm (8 in) intervals. Repeat at the other side of the panel. Baste and machine stitch the layers of fabric in place, using a 1.5 cm (⅝ in) seam allowance.

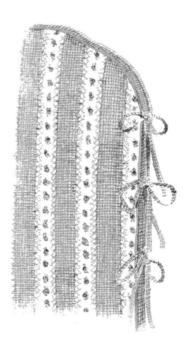

11 Pin the second length of piping along the raw edges of the gusset strip. Insert the remaining ties at the sides, making sure their position corresponds to the ties on the other side of the gusset. Place the back panel right side down over the gusset, piping and ties, aligning the raw edges. Pin, baste and machine sew together, using a 1.5 cm (½ in) seam allowance.

12 Pin, baste and machine stitch a 2 cm (¾ in) hem along the bottom edges of the slipcover. Turn the cover right side out. Attach the headboard to the bed (see Techniques, page 99) and slip the cover over the headboard, tying the bows at the sides.

1 Calculate the size of your headboard (see Techniques, page 99) and cut a piece of plywood to the correct dimensions. Make a template for the shaped outline of the headboard. Cut a piece of paper to the size of the headboard, fold it in half, and mark the outline of one side shoulder and half the central arch. The tallest point of the side shoulder (a) must be three quarters of the height of the central arch (b) and the lowest point (c) half the height. The central arch (d) is a third of the width of the headboard.

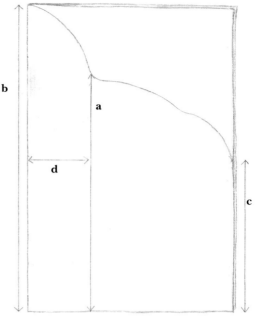

2 Cut out the template. Place it on the plywood and mark around the outline. Using a small saw or jigsaw, cut along the marked line.

3 Use the template to cut a piece of wadding to the same dimensions as the headboard. Glue it to one side of the headboard.

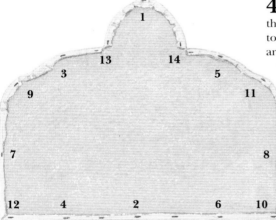

4 Cut two pieces of lining fabric larger than the headboard and pin them right sides together. Put the template on top and draw around it, 5 cm (2 in) from the edges. Cut along the marked line. Place a piece of lining on a flat surface. Put the headboard in the centre of the lining, padded side down, and pull the excess lining to the back of the board. Using a staple gun, staple the lining to the board in the sequence shown. Staple in the gaps and clip the curves.

5 Press in a 6 cm (2½ in) fold to the wrong side all round the second piece of lining. Clip the curves to make the fabric lie flat. Staple the lining to the back of the headboard, covering the raw stapled edges of the front panel of lining.

6 For the slipcover, you will need enough fabric to cover the front and back of the headboard and for a gusset 6 cm (2½ in) deep and the length of the perimeter of the headboard. Add 1.5 cm (⅝ in) seam allowance all round. You will also need enough main fabric to make twelve ties and a piece of piping that is the same length as the gusset.

7 Cut out two panels of fabric for the slip-cover and place them right sides together. Pin the template to the top panel and draw a line around it, 2.5 cm (1 in) away from the edge of the template. Unpin the template and cut along the marked line. Cut out the gusset strip.

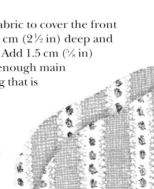

tie-on padding

Tie-on padding is an inexpensive and stylish way of creating
a cosy, comfortable headboard. The concept is extremely simple –
a square of padding is covered in striped cotton and tied to a simple
headboard, creating an inviting and luxurious effect. The beauty
of this idea lies in its versatility – the mood of a bedroom can be
completely transformed in a moment by changing the padded
panel for one covered with a different pattern or colour.

materials & equipment

for the headboard

2 cm (¾ in) thick plywood

upholstery wadding

wood glue

lining fabric

staple gun

wood for struts

for the tie-on padding

upholstery wadding

striped cotton fabric for the slipcover and ties

instructions under flap ➤

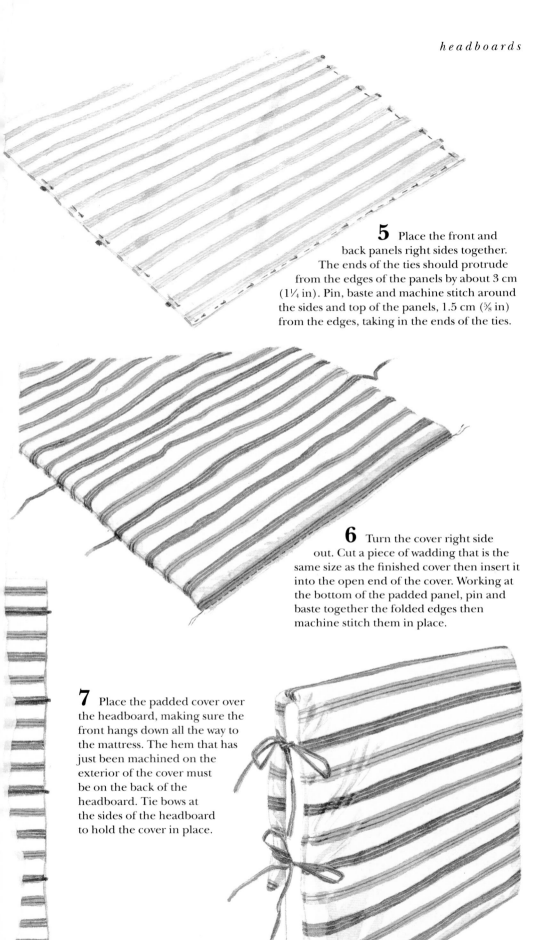

5 Place the front and back panels right sides together. The ends of the ties should protrude from the edges of the panels by about 3 cm (1¼ in). Pin, baste and machine stitch around the sides and top of the panels, 1.5 cm (⅜ in) from the edges, taking in the ends of the ties.

6 Turn the cover right side out. Cut a piece of wadding that is the same size as the finished cover then insert it into the open end of the cover. Working at the bottom of the padded panel, pin and baste together the folded edges then machine stitch them in place.

7 Place the padded cover over the headboard, making sure the front hangs down all the way to the mattress. The hem that has just been machined on the exterior of the cover must be on the back of the headboard. Tie bows at the sides of the headboard to hold the cover in place.

1 Make the headboard (see Techniques, page 99). Cut a piece of upholstery wadding to the same size as the headboard and two pieces of lining fabric, 5 cm (2 in) larger than the headboard all round. Glue the wadding to the front of the headboard. Stretch one piece of lining over the front of the headboard and secure with staples at the back. Press a 5 cm (2 in) fold to the wrong side all around the second piece of lining and staple it to the back of the headboard, covering the raw edges of the lining pulled from the front. Attach the headboard to the bed (see Techniques, page 99).

2 Cut eight strips of fabric, each 4 x 50 cm (1½ x 20 in), and make the ties for the padded panel. Press in a 5 mm (¼ in) fold all around the edges of the strips and fold them in half along the length. Pin, baste and machine stitch along the folded edges.

3 To calculate fabric quantities, measure from the mattress to the top of the headboard and multiply by two. The length of the finished padding will be three quarters of this measurement and the padding must be the width of the headboard. Add 3 cm (1¼ in) seam allowance all around. Cut a front and back panel to these measurements. At one short end of each panel, press in a 2 cm (¾ in) fold to the wrong side. This is now the bottom end.

4 Hang the back panel of the slipcover over the headboard so the raw short edge hangs down the front of the headboard to the mattress and the folded edge is on the back of the headboard. Make two corresponding marks on the panel, 12.5 cm (5 in) down from the top of the headboard, one on the fabric that lies on the front of the headboard and one on the fabric at the back. Now make two more marks 25 cm (10 in) below that, again marking the fabric on each side of the headboard. Lay the back panel on a flat surface, right side up. Place one tie on each mark, and four ties on the marks on the other side of the panel.

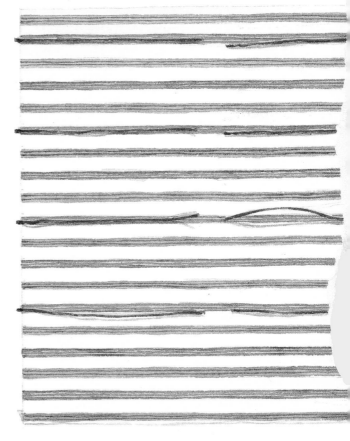

hanging panels

Suspended from wooden pegs, these two hanging panels
provide an easy and attractive alternative to a traditional, firm
headboard. The long panels draw attention to the plump cushions
and invitingly crisp white sheets on the bed below and the narrow
inner borders and boldly striped outer borders create a smart,
tailored effect. The panels would look just as striking
and effective hung above two single beds.

materials & equipment

thick cotton fabric

cotton fabric for the inset border and lining

striped cotton fabric for the outer border

instructions under flap ➤

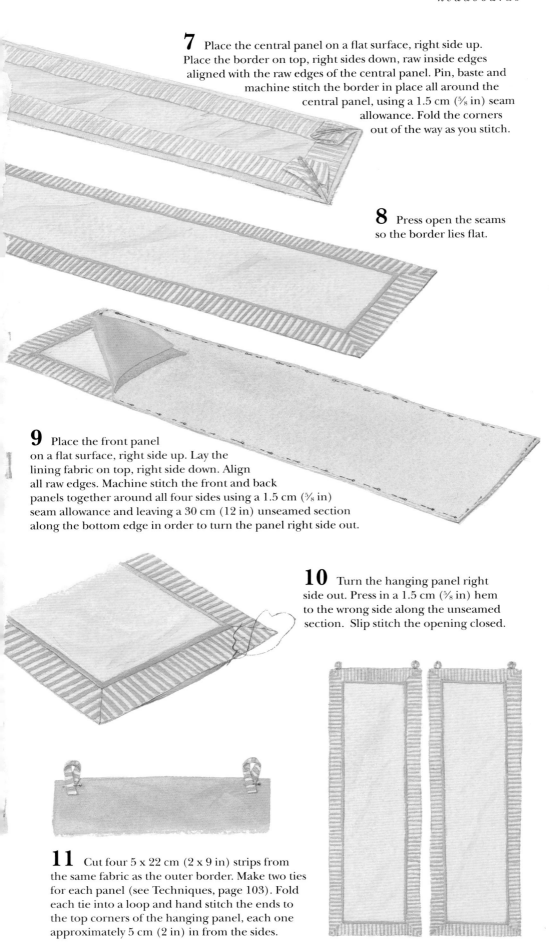

7 Place the central panel on a flat surface, right side up. Place the border on top, right sides down, raw inside edges aligned with the raw edges of the central panel. Pin, baste and machine stitch the border in place all around the central panel, using a 1.5 cm (⅝ in) seam allowance. Fold the corners out of the way as you stitch.

8 Press open the seams so the border lies flat.

9 Place the front panel on a flat surface, right side up. Lay the lining fabric on top, right side down. Align all raw edges. Machine stitch the front and back panels together around all four sides using a 1.5 cm (⅝ in) seam allowance and leaving a 30 cm (12 in) unseamed section along the bottom edge in order to turn the panel right side out.

10 Turn the hanging panel right side out. Press in a 1.5 cm (⅝ in) hem to the wrong side along the unseamed section. Slip stitch the opening closed.

11 Cut four 5 x 22 cm (2 x 9 in) strips from the same fabric as the outer border. Make two ties for each panel (see Techniques, page 103). Fold each tie into a loop and hand stitch the ends to the top corners of the hanging panel, each one approximately 5 cm (2 in) in from the sides.

1 Each finished panel measures 55 cm (22 in) across and 180 cm (6 ft) down. Cut out a central panel measuring 43 x 168 cm (17 ¼ x 67 ¼ in). Also cut out a piece of lining fabric to the size of the finished panel plus 1.5 cm (⅝ in) seam allowance all round.

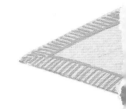

2 For the inset border, cut four strips of fabric, each 5 cm (2 in) deep, two of them 15 cm (6 in) longer than the sides of the central panel and two 15 cm (6 in) wider than the central panel. These measurements include seam allowances.

3 For the outer border, cut four strips of striped fabric, each 10 cm (5 in) deep and exactly the same length as the strips for the inset border. This includes seam allowances.

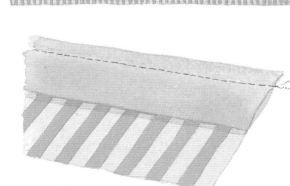

4 To join the inner and outer border fabrics place a long strip of the striped fabric and a strip of correspondingly sized inset fabric right sides together, aligned along one long raw edge. Pin, baste and machine stitch 1.5 cm (⅝ in) from the raw edges. Open out the seam and press. Attach the remaining inner and outer border strips in the same way.

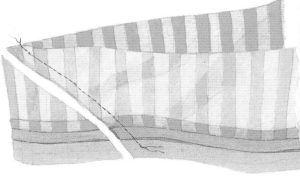

5 Place one short joined strip on top of a long one, right sides together and raw edges aligned. Pin and baste the strips together at a 45° angle running down from the top corner. Check that the angle is correct then machine stitch together, stopping 1.5 cm (⅝ in) from the bottom of the strip. Trim the seams.

6 Attach the other strips in the same way, alternating a long strip with a short one, until the border is complete.

daisy motif headboard

The elegant and unusual outline of this upholstered headboard will add a touch of grandeur to even the smallest bedroom. The headboard has been plumply padded for comfort and then tightly covered with a small-checked cotton fabric. Finally, a daisy motif has been picked out in shiny upholstery tacks.

materials & equipment

2 cm (¾ in) thick plywood for the headboard

upholstery wadding

wood glue

staple gun

heavy cotton fabric

upholstery tacks in a colour to match the main fabric

instructions under flap ➤

5 Place the headboard on a flat surface, wadded side up. Place one piece of the checked fabric on top. Five centimetres (2 in) of fabric will hang over the edges of the headboard all round. Staple the fabric to the front of the board at a few key points to ensure that the front of the headboard is smoothly covered, without any wrinkles or puckering. Put the first staple in the middle of the central arch, a few millimetres (⅛ in) from the edge. Pull the fabric taut and insert the second staple directly beneath the first on the bottom edge of the headboard. Continue in the sequence shown, always keeping the fabric taut.

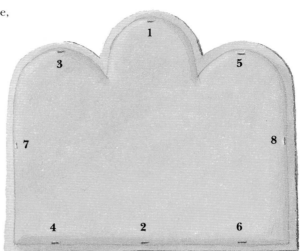

6 To fit the material neatly in between the arches, slit the fabric.

7 Turn the headboard over and pull the surplus fabric to the back of the headboard. Staple the fabric to the headboard.

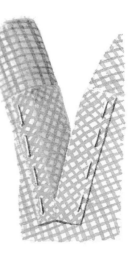

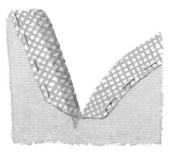

8 If bare patches of plywood can be seen between the arches, take small rectangles of fabric, fold their raw edges under, and staple them over the gaps.

9 Press an 8 cm (3 in) fold in all around the second piece of checked fabric, clipping the curves so the fabric lies flat. Place it on the back of the headboard, so it covers the raw edges of the front panel of fabric. Staple in place.

10 Turn the headboard right side up. Mark out a daisy motif in the centre of the middle arch. Cover the marked outline with closely placed upholstery tacks.

11 Starting at the bottom left-hand corner of the headboard, and working your way all around the perimeter, firmly push in upholstery tacks so that they just touch each other and conceal the staples on the front of the board. Do not tack along the bottom edge of the headboard, as it will not be visible when the headboard is attached to the bed.

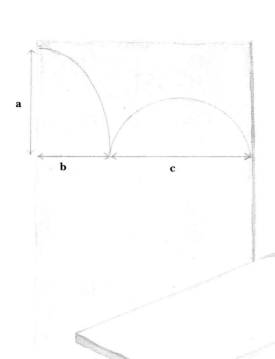

1 Calculate the size of the headboard (see Techniques, page 99) then cut a piece of plywood to the correct dimensions. To make a template for the top of the headboard, cut a piece of paper to the size of the headboard, fold it in half across the width, and mark the outline of one side arch and half the central arch of the headboard. The half central arch must be exactly double the height (a) and half the width (b) of the side arch (c).

2 Cut out the paper template and open it out. Place the plywood on a flat surface and put the template on top. Using a soft pencil, draw all the way around the outline. Remove the template. Using a small saw or jigsaw, carefully cut along the marked line. Smooth any rough edges with sandpaper.

3 Use the paper template to cut out a piece of wadding to exactly the same dimensions as the headboard. Place the wadding on a flat surface and put the template on top. Draw all around the template with pencil or fabric pen, cut out the wadding, and glue it to one side of the headboard.

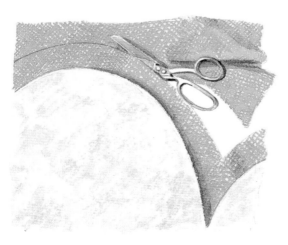

4 You will need enough fabric to cover the front and back of the headboard. Fold the fabric in half, cut it into two pieces and pin right sides together. Place the fabric on a flat surface. Lay the headboard on top and draw a line all around it, approximately 5 cm (2 in) away from the edges of the headboard. Remove the headboard and cut along the marked line. Unpin and separate the two pieces of fabric.

canopies add drama and

romance to a bedroom. Even an ordinary divan can be transformed by the addition of flowing drapes. A corona creates a formal, elegant effect, while a simple mosquito net suspended above the bed will add a hint of colonial style. What could be more soothing than drifting off to sleep cocooned in layers of gently flowing fabric?

left and above A fine organza canopy softens the hard lines of a metal bed. The fabric has been sewn to a hoop that is suspended from the ceiling. A narrow gold velvet ribbon is stitched to the outside edges of the canopy, adding a touch of luxury to a cool white scheme. The crisp white cotton bed linen is edged in matching gold ribbon, unifying the scheme.
right A magnificent Shaker cherrywood fourposter is adorned with a panel of bold checks and subtle stripes, loosely knotted to a horizontal support. The practical ties mean that the panel can be easily removed for seasonal changes or laundering.

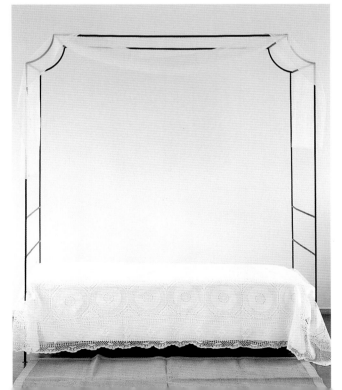

left and above A modern metal fourposter with clean minimalist lines is softened with delicate drapery made from hemmed organza and an intricate lace bedspread, which create an ethereal feel without concealing the elegant lines of the bed.

scalloped corona

A corona brings a regal and elegant air to any bed, and has the ability to transform the most ordinary of bedrooms into a luxurious retreat. The elegant carved-wood corona shown in the picture below is a traditional Swedish design. Similar ready-made coronas can be difficult to find, so here I show how to create the effect using a corona board made from plywood and concealed by a scalloped pelmet, which adds a majestic finishing touch.

materials & equipment

2 cm (¾ in) thick plywood for the corona board

angled brackets

flexible curtain track

curtain hooks

woven checked cotton fabric

2.5 cm (1 in) wide gathering tape

2 cm (¾ in) wide velcro

instructions under flap ➤

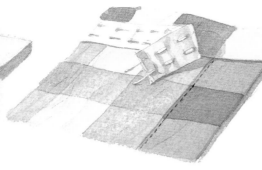

8 At the top of the curtain, press a 3 cm (1¼ in) fold over to the right side. Pin and baste in place. Place the heading tape over the fold, 2 cm (¾ in) below the top folded edge of the curtain, so the turnover of fabric is concealed. Pin, baste and machine stitch the heading tape in place, folding under the raw edges at each end.

9 Pull the strings in the tape to gather the curtain. Knot the ends. Insert curtain hooks into the heading tape then hang the curtain from the track. Mark the hem level with pins, take down the curtain and fold up a double hem. Press and rehang the curtain.

10 For the pelmet cut two pieces of fabric to the width of the curved front of the board and 40 cm (16 in) deep plus a 1.5 cm (⅜ in) seam allowance all round.

11 Make a scallop template for the pelmet (see Templates, page 104). The scallop should be twice as deep as it is wide.

12 Pin the two pelmet panels right sides together. Place the template on top, draw around it, then cut out the fabric.

13 Pin, baste and machine stitch the two panels together around the side and scalloped edges, using a 1.5 cm (⅜ in) seam allowance. Clip the curves and turn right side out.

14 Press in a 1.5 cm (⅜ in) fold along the open top edges of the pelmet. Pin, baste and slip stitch the edges together.

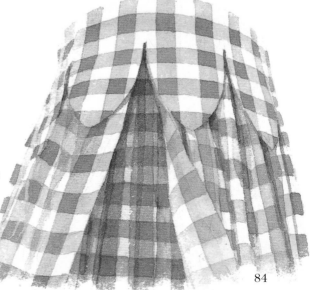

15 Take the strip of velcro that corresponds to the velcro on the corona board and pin, baste and machine stitch it to the top of the pelmet, 1 cm (½ in) below the edge. Press the velcro on the pelmet to the velcro on the corona board to hang in place.

1 Make a template for the corona board. Draw an exact semicircle with a compass and increase it to the desired size on a photocopier. Cut out the template, place it on a piece of plywood and draw around the outline. Cut along the marked line with a small saw.

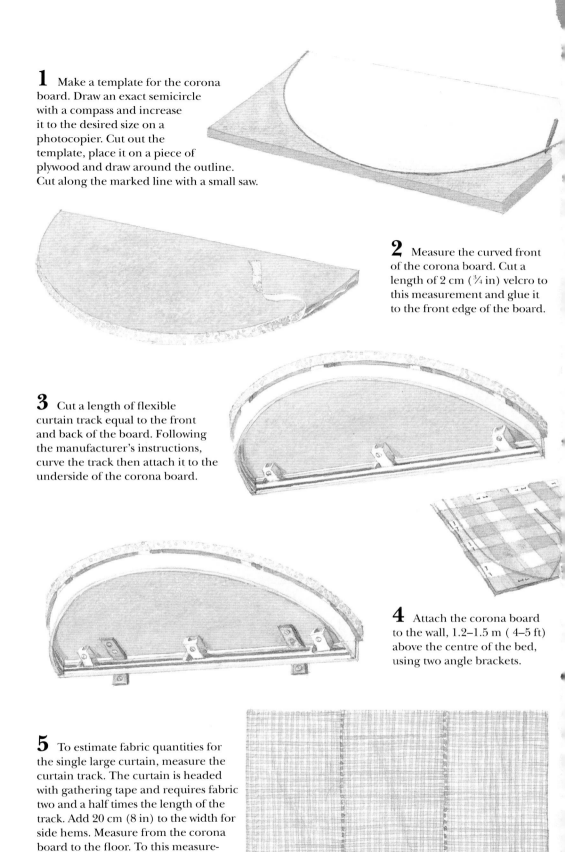

2 Measure the curved front of the corona board. Cut a length of 2 cm (¾ in) velcro to this measurement and glue it to the front edge of the board.

3 Cut a length of flexible curtain track equal to the front and back of the board. Following the manufacturer's instructions, curve the track then attach it to the underside of the corona board.

4 Attach the corona board to the wall, 1.2–1.5 m (4–5 ft) above the centre of the bed, using two angle brackets.

5 To estimate fabric quantities for the single large curtain, measure the curtain track. The curtain is headed with gathering tape and requires fabric two and a half times the length of the track. Add 20 cm (8 in) to the width for side hems. Measure from the corona board to the floor. To this measurement add 50 cm (20 in) so the curtains will swag over the sides of the bed plus 13 cm (5 in) for hem and heading.

6 Cut out the fabric and join widths using a French seam (see Techniques, page 102). At the sides, press in a double 5 cm (2 in) hem to the right side. Pin, baste and machine stitch in place.

7 Cut a strip of gathering tape to the width of the curtain plus 3 cm (1¼ in) at each end. Knot the strings at one end of the tape and leave them loose at the other.

voile bed canopy

This simple arrangement in floaty flowered voile brings an
air of romance and elegance to a bedroom without looking too
fussy and flouncy. Although the effect is dramatic, the bed canopy
is surprisingly easy to create. Abundant quantities of voile cascade
gently from a short length of curtain pole that has been attached
to the wall with a bracket and finished with an unobtrusive finial,
which keeps the gathered voile in place.

materials & equipment

floral voile

plain cotton for lining

short wooden curtain pole with bracket and finial

instructions under flap ➤

7 Fold the length of material in half across the width, so the lining is right sides together. Baste the material together a few centimetres (½–1 in) below the fold to prevent it from slipping.

8 Lay the folded voile flat. Using fabric pen, mark two parallel lines across the width of the voile, the first line 5 cm (2 in) beneath the folded edge and the second another 3 cm (1¼ in) beneath that. Pin above the top line then machine stitch along the marked line across the full width of the fabric. Repeat for the lower line. The voile and lining are now joined, and a casing of fabric has been formed.

9 Take down the pole and insert it into the casing, evenly ruffling the voile. Slot the finial on to the end of the pole to hold the canopy in place.

1 Centre the bracket above your bed and attach it to the wall. Slot the pole into the bracket and measure from the top of the pole to the floor. Add 1 m (3 ft) to this measurement, plus 20 cm (8 in) for the heading and 8 cm (3 in) for the hem. Double this measurement for your final length of fabric. One width of fabric is sufficient.

2 Take your length of floral voile, fold in it half across the width, and cut in two. Place the two pieces on a flat surface, right sides together. Pin, baste and machine stitch the two pieces of voile together 2 cm (¾ in) below the top raw edge.

3 Cut out a length of lining to the same length as the whole piece of floral voile. Do not cut it into equal lengths. Instead fold it in half across the width and press.

4 Press a double 1 cm (½ in) hem to the wrong side all the way down the sides of the voile panels. Pin, baste and machine stitch in place. Press a double 4 cm (1¾ in) hem to the wrong side along the bottom edges. Mitre the corners. Pin, baste and machine stitch in place.

5 Hem the lining fabric as described in step 4, but turn up a double 8 cm (3 in) hem to the wrong side along the bottom edges, so the lining is slightly shorter than the voile.

6 Place the joined floral panels on a flat surface, right side down. Place the lining panel on top, right side up, so that the wrong sides are together. Align the seam line on the floral fabric with the pressed fold in the lining fabric. Pin then baste the lining and voile together along this line.

tie-on bed curtains

Four-posters are often associated with grand, formal bed-dressings, but here the austere lines of a very contemporary metal-framed four-poster are softened by eight cotton bed curtains loosely tied to the top of the bed frame. As both sides of the hangings are visible, a woven check fabric has been used to dispense with the need for lining.

materials & equipment

thick checked Madras cotton

bias binding in a contrasting colour

instructions under flap ➤

5 When the binding is stitched in place all around the curtain, press the seam out flat.

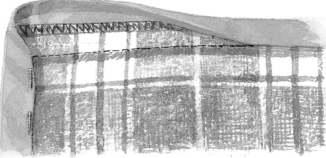

6 Turn the curtain over and fold the pressed edge of the binding to the wrong side of the curtain.

7 Pin and baste the binding in place all around the curtain, folding the corners in as neatly and unobtrusively as you can. Slip stitch to secure.

8 A total of 40 ties are needed, five for each curtain. Cut 40 strips of binding, each 4 x 40 cm (1¾ x 16 in), and make the ties (see Techniques, page 103).

9 Take five ties. Fold them in half and press. Position a tie in each top corner of the curtain and space the others at regular intervals in between. Pin each tie to the back of the binding at the halfway crease. Machine stitch the ties in place.

10 Repeat steps 3 to 9 to make the remaining seven curtains. With loose bows, tie a pair of curtains to each side of the bed frame and a pair at the head and end of the bed.

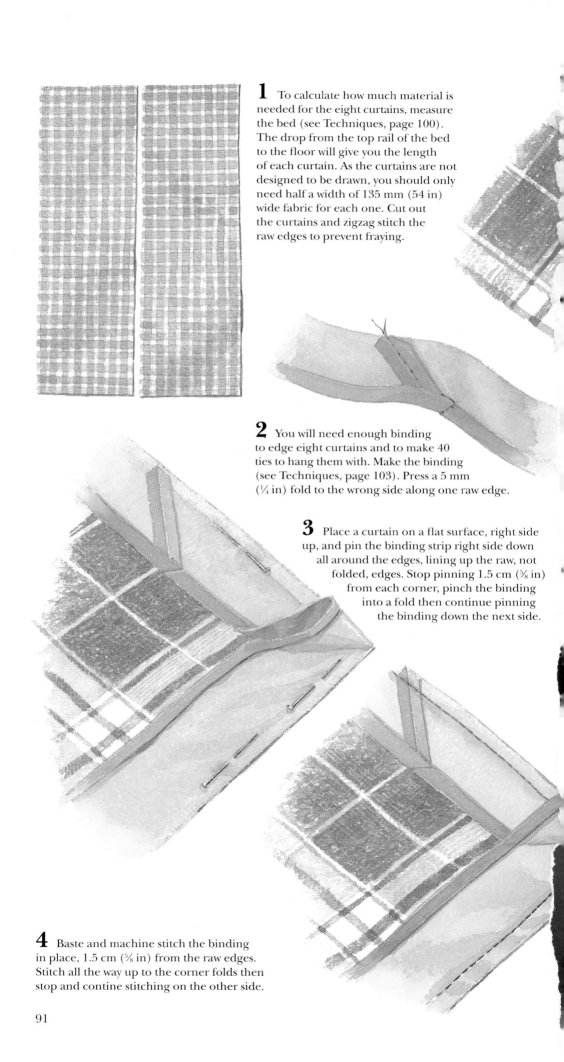

1 To calculate how much material is needed for the eight curtains, measure the bed (see Techniques, page 100). The drop from the top rail of the bed to the floor will give you the length of each curtain. As the curtains are not designed to be drawn, you should only need half a width of 135 mm (54 in) wide fabric for each one. Cut out the curtains and zigzag stitch the raw edges to prevent fraying.

2 You will need enough binding to edge eight curtains and to make 40 ties to hang them with. Make the binding (see Techniques, page 103). Press a 5 mm (¼ in) fold to the wrong side along one raw edge.

3 Place a curtain on a flat surface, right side up, and pin the binding strip right side down all around the edges, lining up the raw, not folded, edges. Stop pinning 1.5 cm (⅜ in) from each corner, pinch the binding into a fold then continue pinning the binding down the next side.

4 Baste and machine stitch the binding in place, 1.5 cm (⅜ in) from the raw edges. Stitch all the way up to the corner folds then stop and contine stitching on the other side.

striped canopy

This scalloped bed canopy, with its bold blocks of primary colour, is designed to hang over the frame of a four-poster bed. It has a pleasing simplicity that complements the robust lines of this Shaker-style wooden four-poster perfectly. The central panel that forms the roof of the canopy is made from unlined white linen. The scalloped valance is lined and hangs down around all four sides of the bed frame, lending sufficient weight to hold the whole canopy in place.

materials & equipment

white linen

coloured linen

lining fabric

instructions under flap ➤

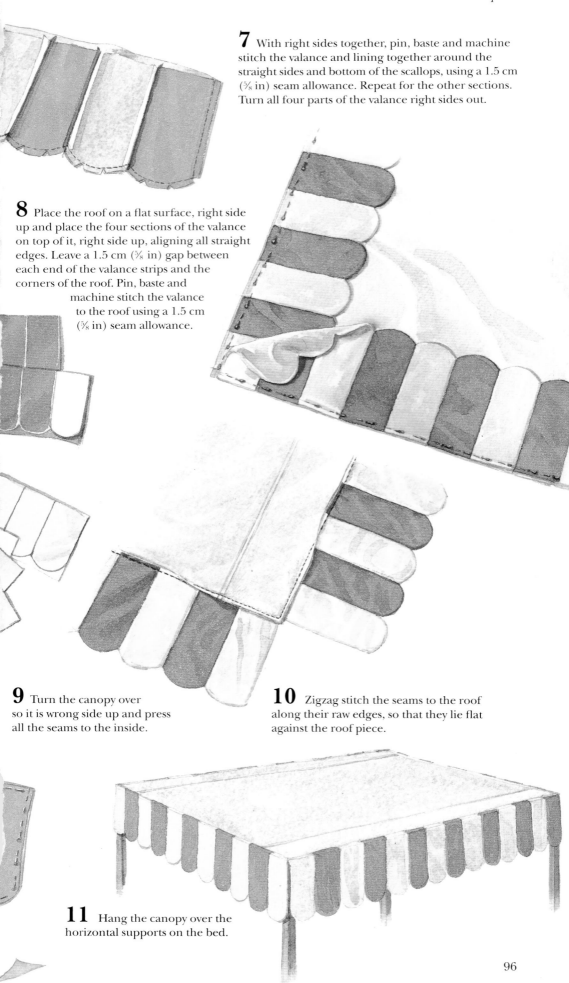

7 With right sides together, pin, baste and machine stitch the valance and lining together around the straight sides and bottom of the scallops, using a 1.5 cm (⅝ in) seam allowance. Repeat for the other sections. Turn all four parts of the valance right sides out.

8 Place the roof on a flat surface, right side up and place the four sections of the valance on top of it, right side up, aligning all straight edges. Leave a 1.5 cm (⅝ in) gap between each end of the valance strips and the corners of the roof. Pin, baste and machine stitch the valance to the roof using a 1.5 cm (⅝ in) seam allowance.

9 Turn the canopy over so it is wrong side up and press all the seams to the inside.

10 Zigzag stitch the seams to the roof along their raw edges, so that they lie flat against the roof piece.

11 Hang the canopy over the horizontal supports on the bed.

96

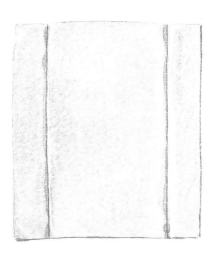

1 To calculate how much material is needed for the roof of the canopy, measure the length and width of the frame from just inside the horizontal supports. Add a 1.5 cm (⅝ in) seam allowance all round.

2 Cut out the linen panels for the roof of the canopy and join widths if necessary, using a full width panel in the middle, flanked by two narrower panels of equal width (see Techniques, page 100). Join the panels using a flat fell seam (see Techniques, page 102).

3 Make a template for the scallops (see Templates, page 104). Enlarge the template until the scallop is 19 cm (7½ in) wide. This measurement includes a 1.5 cm (⅝ in) seam allowance all around the scallop.

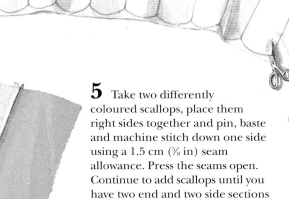

4 The finished width of each scallop is 16 cm (6½ in). To work out how many scallops are needed, divide the length and width of the bed frame by 16 (6½). Pin the template to the fabric, mark around it, and cut out the scallops. Make sure you have an equal number of red and white scallops.

5 Take two differently coloured scallops, place them right sides together and pin, baste and machine stitch down one side using a 1.5 cm (⅝ in) seam allowance. Press the seams open. Continue to add scallops until you have two end and two side sections that are the required length.

6 Cut out four strips of lining fabric to the same measurements as the valance sides and ends. Place the valance on the lining, right sides together. Pin the two pieces of fabric together and cut around the scalloped bottom of the valance so the lining is exactly the same size and shape as the valance.

equipment and techniques

Basic equipment

To make the projects in this book you will need some basic tools. A pair of good quality cutting shears is essential, as are some medium-sized dressmaker's scissors and small embroidery scissors. Equally important are a metal tape measure, steel metre rule and a small plastic ruler, which will enable you to measure up accurately and to double check all measurements. Invest in some good quality steel dressmaking pins, which will not rust, and keep them in a box so they stay sharp. A steam iron will prove invaluable during the making up process, but should be used with a damp cloth to protect delicate fabrics. When marking up fabrics, vanishing fabric pens are easy to apply and the ink fades away after 72 hours. A metal thimble is another useful item, as is a knitting needle to coax ties right side out.

Some of the projects in this book involve making a headboard from plywood. To cut the plywood to the required shape, you will need a small saw, and fabric glue is necessary to attach padding or lining to the board. Securing fabric to a headboard may require the use of a heavy duty staple gun. You will also need a hammer, a drill and an assortment of nails and screws for hanging drapes and coronas or attaching headboards to beds.

The projects in this book involve both hand and machine sewing and a sewing machine is needed to make most items. Although it is possible to make many of the items featured by hand, it would be a long and laborious process. Your sewing machine should have a good range of basic stitches. Sophisticated accessories are not necessary, but a piping foot is required for some of the projects in the book.

Finally, the process of making bed linen will be much easier and more enjoyable if you are able to work in a well-lit, well-ventilated area and have access to a large worktable.

Choosing fabric

For each project the fabrics are specified, as the weight, texture and pattern is suited to the particular design. If you want to choose an alternative material, always try to select fabric of a similar weight. Check that your chosen fabric is preshrunk and fade-resistant.

Before you cut into the fabric, check it carefully for any flaws. Some minor flaws can sometimes be hidden in hems or seams. If the fabric is badly flawed, return it to the manufacturer or retailer.

You will find cleaning instructions printed on the selvedges of most fabrics in the form of care symbols. Any lined items should always be dry cleaned, as lining fabric and main fabric tend to shrink at different rates when washed.

The fire-retardant qualities of furnishing fabrics are governed by legislation in most countries. We suggest that you obtain advice from a retailer to ensure that your chosen fabric is in line with these regulations.

Measuring up for bed linen

Before you embark on any of the projects in this book, you must first accurately measure the bed that the item is intended to furnish. This is essential as it will enable you to calculate the size of the finished item and work out how much fabric you will need to make it. Always take measurements with a steel tape measure (plastic ones can stretch and become inaccurate) and enlist the help of an assistant if the bed is a large one.

Measuring up for a pillowcase
Measure the width and length of the pillow. Add 26 cm (10 ¼ in) flap and seam allowance to the width and 3 cm (1 ¼ in) to the length, unless otherwise stated in a project.

Measuring up for a duvet cover
Measure the width and length of the duvet and add 5 cm (2 in) to each measurement.

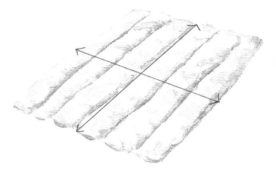

Measuring up for a bedspread
Measure the bed with bedclothes and pillows in place. For the length, measure from the bedhead to the floor at the foot of the bed. Add an extra 30 cm (12 in) to tuck behind the pillows. For the width, measure from the floor on one side of the bed over the bed to the floor on the other side. Seam allowances are given in the individual projects.

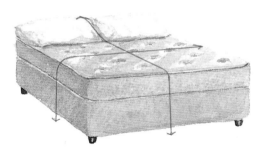

Measuring up for a valance
Measure the bed base without the mattress. For the length of the central panel (which lies beneath the mattress) measure the head to the foot of the bed. For the width, measure from one side of the bed base to the other. For the depth of the skirt, measure from the top of the bed base to the floor. The amount of fabric required for the skirt will depend on the fullness of the valance. Seam allowances are given in the individual projects.

Measuring up for a headboard
In order to calculate the width of the headboard, you must first measure the width of the bed. The headboard must be the same width as the bed from side edge to side edge. It should be approximately 1 m (3 ft) tall, but the height and shape of the headboard can be adjusted, depending on the effect you wish to achieve. Take into account the size of your bed – a tiny bed may need a lower headboard, and vice versa.

Making a headboard
Cut a piece of plywood to the required proportions and smooth any rough edges with sandpaper. For a shaped headboard, you will have to make a template and scale it up to the desired size (see Templates, page 104). Cut a piece of paper or card to the size of the headboard and draw, trace or photocopy the desired shape on to the paper. Cut out the template and attach it to the headboard. Draw all around it with a pencil or marker pen then cut all along the marked line, using a small saw.
Cover the headboard in lining or in main fabric and attach it to the bed with two strips of wood, each about 7.5 cm (3 in) wide and 2.5 cm (1 in) thick. Saw a long notch in one end of each strip so it will slot over the screws on the back of the bed base. Measure the distance between these screws so you will know how far apart to fix the wooden strips.

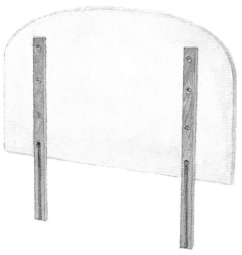

Measuring up for bed hangings and curtains

If you have a four-poster bed, measure the drop from the bottom of the horizontal supports to the floor for the length of the bedhangings, and the distance between the vertical supports for the width.

If you wish to make a corona or other wall-mounted bed draperies, it is much easier to measure up and calculate fabric quantities once the pole or corona board is fixed in place. As a rough guide, they should be positioned approximately 30 cm (12 in) below the ceiling but this measurement may have to be adjusted, depending on the proportions of the room. Fix any fittings securely to the wall, using sturdy brackets that will be able to bear the weight of the fitting plus several metres of fabric.

Cutting out the fabric

When making bed linen, or indeed any soft furnishings, it is essential that fabric is cut straight, or the finished item will hang crookedly. Unroll or unfold the fabric on a flat surface. Use a set square and metal ruler to mark a straight line in pencil or fabric pen across the width on the wrong side of the fabric.

To cut a width of fabric in half, fold it selvedge to selvedge then press. Carefully cut along the pressed fold line. If you are using fabric with a high sheen or pile, mark the top of each width with a notch so you can ensure that all the fabric will run in the right direction on the finished item.

Joining widths

When making duvets, sheets and bedspreads, always place a full width panel in the centre of the item with equal part or whole widths joined on either side.

To join widths, place one width on top of another, right sides facing, and pin, baste and machine stitch the widths together, using a straight 1.5 cm (⅜ in) seam. Trim away any surplus fabric and clip the seams to prevent any puckering or bunching.

Matching patterns

To match patterns across several widths of fabric, fold under a 1.5 cm (⅜ in) seam allowance on one width of fabric and press. Place the other width on a flat surface, right side up. Take the width with the folded edge and place it on top of the second width of fabric. Match up the pattern. Fold the top piece of fabric so the two pieces are right sides together then seam down the fold line. Open the seam and press flat.

BASIC SEWING TECHNIQUES

Stitches

Basting stitch

This temporary stitch holds fabric in place until it is permanently secured. Knot the end of the thread and take large loose stitches. Use a brightly coloured thread so the basting is easy to spot and can be removed quickly after the permanent stitching has been done.

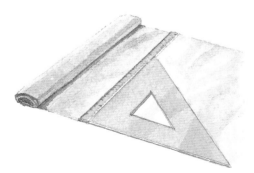

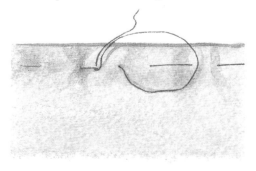

Slip stitch

Slip stitch holds a folded edge to flat fabric or two folded edges together, as in a mitred corner. Work on the wrong side of the fabric from right to left. Start with the needle in the fold. Push it out and pick up a few threads from the flat fabric, then insert it into the hem again, all in one continuous movement. The stitches should be almost invisible.

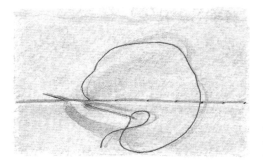

Herringbone stitch

This stitch is used to hold a raw edge to flat fabric. Work from left to right on the wrong side of the fabric. Start with the needle in the fold of the hem. Push it through the fold fabric and bring the needle diagonally up to the flat fabric. Take a small backward stitch in the flat fabric, approximately 5 mm (¼ in) above the fold, picking up a couple of threads. Bring the needle diagonally back down to the fold and make a small backward stitch of equal size to the previous one through one thickness of the fabric.

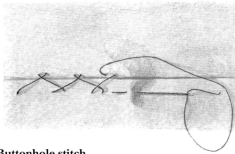

Buttonhole stitch

This stitch is both decorative and strengthening as it prevents the buttonhole from fraying. It can also be used wherever a raw edge needs to be neatened or secured. Work on the right side of the fabric, using a short needle and a strong thread with a knotted end. Stitch with the raw edge uppermost. Push the needle through the fabric, from back to front, approximately 3 mm (⅛ in) below the raw edge of the buttonhole. Twist the thread around the tip of the needle then pull the needle through to form a knot at the raw edge of the fabric. Always keep the stitches evenly spaced. Some sewing machines have a very useful buttonhole attachment.

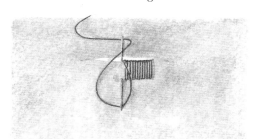

Feather stitch

This decorative stitch should be worked in silk embroidery thread on the right side of the fabric. It is easiest to do if you are following a straight line, such as a seam, and can imagine that there is a parallel line about 5 mm (¼ in) above and below the seam. Bring the needle through the fabric at A and insert it into the fabric at B. Bring it out again at C, looping the thread under the needle before pulling it through. Repeat the process by inserting the needle again at D, emerging again at E, then looping the thread beneath the needle again. Continue to repeat this pattern, always alternating the looped stitches to alternate sides of the central line.

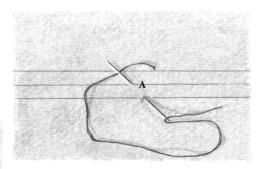

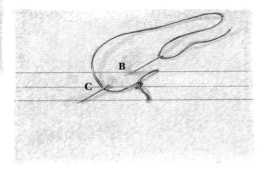

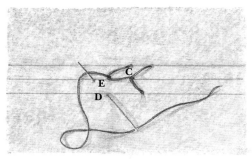

Seams

Flat seam

This seam is used to join pieces of fabric. Place the two pieces of fabric right sides together, aligning the edges that are to be seamed. Pin and baste then machine stitch the seam. Reverse the stitches at the beginning and end of the seam to secure it in place. Press the seam flat against the wrong side of the material for a neat finish.

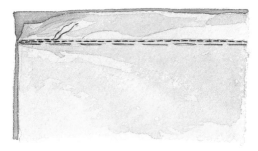

Flat fell seam

This is a sturdy seam for joining heavy fabric. Join two pieces of fabric with a flat seam. Press the seam to one side. Trim the underneath seam to half its width. Fold the upper seam allowance over the trimmed one and baste. Machine stitch a second seam all the way along the folded edge.

French seam

This self-neatening seam contains all raw edges and is used to join sheers and other lightweight fabrics. Place two pieces of fabric wrong sides together, aligning the raw edges that are to be seamed. Pin, baste and machine stitch a narrow seam close to the raw edge. Trim the seam allowance. Fold the material right sides together and pin, baste and machine stitch a second seam 1 cm (⅜ in) from the first, enclosing all raw edges in a narrow tube of fabric.

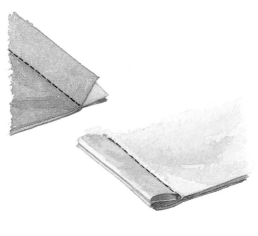

Double hem

A double hem encloses raw edges and lies flat against the back of fabric. For a 10 cm (4 in) double hem, the hem allowance will be 20 cm (8 in). Press in the hem allowance along the edge of the fabric. Open out the hem and fold the raw edge up to the pressed line. Fold up again and secure in place.

Mitring corners

Mitring is the neatest and tidiest way of working hem corners. Press in the hem allowance along the bottom and sides of the fabric then open it out flat again. Where the two fold lines meet, turn in the corner of the fabric diagonally. Turn in the hems along the pressed fold to form a neat diagonal line. Use slip stitch to secure.

Making an angled mitre

An angled mitre is necessary when a double bottom hem is wider than the side hems. Press in the hem allowances then open out again. Fold in the corner towards the bottom hem. Then make the first fold in the double hem. Fold in the side hem then make the second fold in the double hem. The folded edges should meet.

Making bias binding

Bias binding is an effective and attractive way to enclose raw edges of fabric. It is available ready made in a wide range of colours, but it is quick and easy to make your own. Place your chosen fabric on a flat surface, wrong side up. Diagonally fold in one corner of the fabric until the end is aligned with the selvedge, forming a triangle of fabric. The diagonal fold line is the bias line of the fabric. Mark strips parallel to the bias line all the way across the fabric and cut them out.

Join the strips to make one continous strip of bias binding. Place two strips right sides together at right angles, lining up the raw edges. Pin and machine stitch across the width, using a 7.5 mm ($\frac{1}{4}$ in) seam allowance. Trim the seams, press flat and trim the corners.

Making ties and tabs

To make a tie, cut a strip of material to the desired width and length. Fold the strip in half along the length, wrong sides together, and press. Pin, baste and machine sew all along the long side and one short end. Leave one end unstitched. Push the tie right side out with the aid of a knitting needle. Turn in a 5 mm ($\frac{1}{4}$ in) fold to the inside of the tie, press in place, and slip stitch the end closed. Tabs can be made in exactly the same way as ties – the only difference is that the strip of fabric is wider and they are generally buttoned, not tied.

Making piping

Piping is made from a length of piping cord covered with bias binding. The binding must be wide enough to cover the cord and to allow a 1.5 cm ($\frac{5}{8}$ in) seam allowance to either side of it. Place the cord in the middle of the wrong side of the binding and wrap the binding so the cord is enclosed. Baste close to the cord. Machine stitch close to the cord using a piping foot.

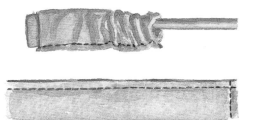

templates

All the templates in this book must be enlarged. Either use a photocopier to enlarge the template to the desired proportions (sometimes stated in the individual project) on stiff paper or card, or trace the pattern on to graph paper, increase the proportions to the desired size then trace on to stiff paper or card. Cut out the template. Pin it to the wrong side of the fabric then mark all the way around the outline of the template in vanishing fabric pen.

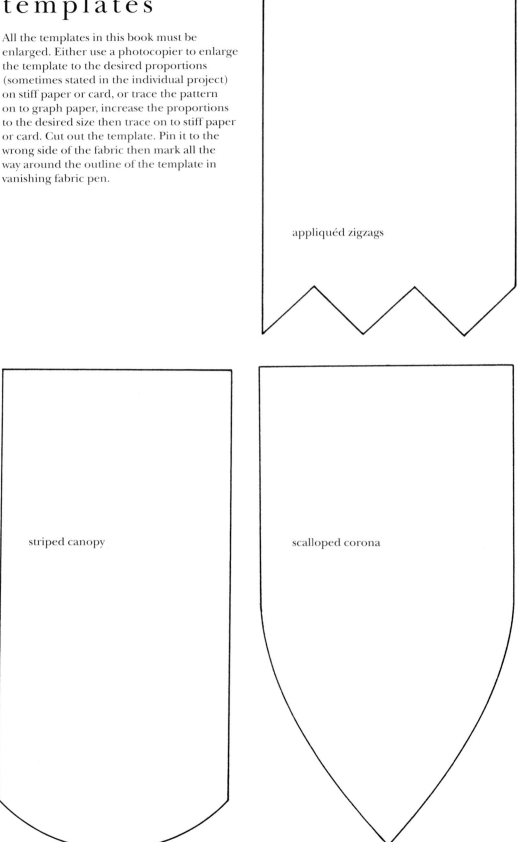

appliquéd zigzags

striped canopy

scalloped corona

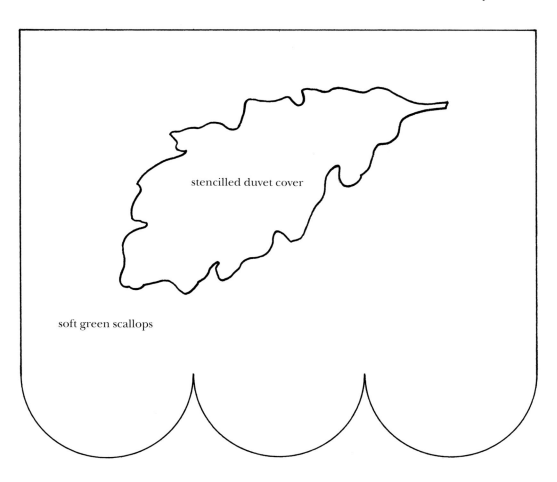

stencilled duvet cover

soft green scallops

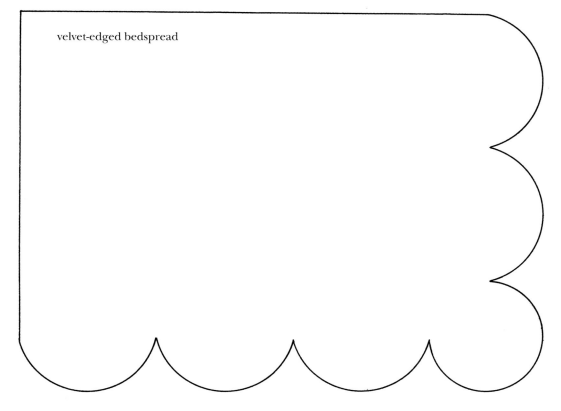

velvet-edged bedspread

directory of suppliers

fabrics

*Abbott & Boyd
Chelsea Garden Market,
London SW10 0XE

*Altfield
Chelsea Harbour Design
Centre, London SW10 0XE

*Alton-Brooke/Brooke London
5 Sleaford Street
London SW8 5AB

Anta Scotland
Fearn, Tain, Ross-shire
Scotland IV20 TL

Laura Ashley
27 Bagleys Lane
London SW6 2AR

Baer & Ingram
273 Wandsworth Bridge Rd
London SW6 2TX

G.P. & J. Baker
Decorative Fabrics Gallery
278-80 Brompton Road
London SW3 2AS

Beaumont & Fletcher
261 Fulham Road
London SW3 6HY

*Bennison
16 Holbein Place
London SW1 8NL

Celia Birtwell
71 Westbourne Park Road
London W2 5QH

The Blue Door
74 Church Road
London SW13 0DQ

*Borderline
Chelsea Harbour Design
Centre, London SW10 0XE

*Brunschwig & Fils
Chelsea Harbour Design
Centre, London SW10 0XE

*Busby & Busby
63 Salisbury Street,
Blandford, Dorset DT11 7PY

Nina Campbell
9 Walton Street
London SW3 2JD

*Manuel Canovas
2 North Terrace
Brompton Road
London SW3 2BA

*Chase Erwin
Chelsea Garden Market
Chelsea Harbour
London SW10 0XE

Chelsea Textiles
7 Walton Street
London SW3 2JD

Jane Churchill-Wish
151 Sloane Street
London SW3 9BZ

*Claremont
29 Elyston Place
London SW3 3NT

Colefax & Fowler
39 Brook Street
London W1Y 2JE

*Wendy Cushings Trimmings
Chelsea Garden Market
Chelsea Harbour
London SW10 0XE

Thomas Dare
341 Kings Road
London SW3 5ES

Design Archives
Decorative Fabrics Gallery
278-80 Brompton Road
London SW3 2AS

Designers Guild
277 Kings Road
London SW3 5EN

*Donghia
Chelsea Harbour Design
Centre, London SW10 0XE

*Jason D'Souza
Chelsea Harbour Design
Centre, London SW10 0XE

*Guy Evans
96 Great Titchfield Street
London W1P 7 AG

Firifiss
Decorative Fabrics Gallery
278-80 Brompton Road
London SW3 2AS

Timney Fowler
388 Kings Road
London SW3 5UZ

*Mary Fox Linton
Chelsea Harbour Design
Centre, London SW10 0XE

Anna French
343 Kings Road
London SW3 5ES

*Pierre Frey and Braquenié
251-53 Fulham Road
London SW3 6HY

Habitat
196 Tottenham Court Road
London W1P 9LD

Harrods
Knightsbridge
London SW1X 7XL

*Hill & Knowles
Chelsea Harbour Design
Centre, London SW10 0XE

Hodsoll McKenzie
52 Pimlico Road
London SW1W 8LP

Housemade
157 Munster Road
London SW6 6DA

Ikea
2 Drury Way
North Circular Road
London NW10 0TH

*JAB International
Chelsea Harbour Design
Centre, London SW10 0XE

KA International
60 Sloane Avenue
London SW3 3DD

Cath Kidston
8 Clarendon Cross
London W11 4AP

⊡ Knickerbean
PO Box 36, Thetford
Norfolk IP24 2TT

Ralph Lauren Home
Harvey Nichols
109-25 Knightsbridge London
SW1X 7RJ

*Lee Jofa
Chelsea Harbour Design
Centre, London SW10 0XE
*Lelièvre
101 Cleveland Street
London W1P 5PN
John Lewis Partnership
Oxford Street
London W1A 1EX
Lewis & Wood
48a Pimlico Road
London SW1W 8LP
Liberty
210 Regent Street
London W1R 6AH
McCulloch & Wallis
25 Dering Street
London W1R 0BH
*McKinney & Co.
1 Wandon Road
London SW6 2JF
*Malabar Cotton Company
31-33 South Bank
Business Centre
Ponton Road
London SW8 5BL
◰ Ian Mankin
109 Regents Park Road
London NW1 8UR
Monkwell
Decorative Fabrics Gallery
278-80 Brompton Road
London SW3 2AS
*Christopher Moore Textiles
1 Munro Terrace
Cheyne Walk
London SW10 0DL
Mulberry Home
76 Chelsea Manor Street
London SW3 5QE
Henry Newbery
Trimmings
18 Newman Street
London W1P 4AB
*Nobilis Fontan
Chelsea Harbour Design
Centre, London SW10 0XE
◰ Old Town
32 Elm Hill
Norwich NR3 1HG
Osborne & Little
304-8 Kings Road
London SW3 5UH
*Paper Moon
54 Fairfax Road
London NW6 4EL
Parkertex
Decorative Fabrics Gallery
278-80 Brompton Road
London SW3 2AS
*Percheron
Chelsea Harbour Design
Centre, London SW10 0XE
*Pongees
28-30 Hoxton Square
London N1 6NN
Pukkah Palace
174 Tower Bridge Road
London SE1 3LR

*Ramm, Son & Crocker
Chelsea Harbour Design
Centre, London SW10 0XE
V. V. Rouleaux
10 Symons Street
London SW3 2TJ
*Sahco Hesslein
Chelsea Harbour Design
Centre, London SW10 0XE
Sanderson
112-20 Brompton Road
London SW3 1JJ
*Ian Sanderson
Chelsea Harbour Design
Centre, London SW10 0XE
◰ Shaker
322 Kings Road
London SW3 0DU
George Spencer
4 West Halkin Street
London SW1X 8JA
John Stefanidis
7 Chelsea Manor Street
London SW3 3TW
F. R. Street
Frederick House, Harrison Way
Wickford Business Park
Wickford, Essex SS11 8XB
*Tissunique
Chelsea Harbour Design
Centre, London SW10 0XE
*Titley & Marr
Chelsea Harbour Design
Centre, London SW10 0XE
Today Interiors
Hollis Road, Grantham
Lincolnshire NG31 7QH
*Bruno Triplet
Chelsea Harbour Design
Centre, London SW10 0XE
*Turnell & Gigon
Chelsea Harbour Design
Centre, London SW10 0XE
*Warner Fabrics
Chelsea Harbour Design
Centre, London SW10 0XE
*Watts of Westminster
Chelsea Harbour Design
Centre, London SW10 0XE
*Brian Yates
Chelsea Harbour Design
Centre, London SW10 0XE
*Zimmer & Rohde
Chelsea Harbour Design
Centre, London SW10 0XE
*Zoffany
Chelsea Harbour Design
Centre, London SW10 0XE

beds, bed linen and accessories

And So to Bed
638 Kings Road
London SW6 2PU
The Blue Door
74 Church Road
London SW13 0DQ
◰ Cologne & Cotton
74 Regent Street

Leamington Spa,
Warwickshire CV32 4NS
The Conran Shop
81 Fulham Road
London SW3 6RD
Cover Up Designs of Kingsclere
9 Kingsclere Park
Kingsclere, Newbury
Bucks RG20 4SW
The Cross
141 Portland Road
London W11 4LR
Damask
3 & 4 Broxholme House
New Kings Road
London SW6 4AA
J & M Davidson
62 Ledbury Road
London W11 2AJ
The Easy Chair
30 Lyndhurst Road
Worthing, Sussex BN11 2DF
The Eiderdown Studio
228 Withycombe Village Rd
Exmouth, Devon EX8 3BD
Nicole Fabre
592 Kings Road
London SW6 2DX
Harriet Ann Sleigh Beds
Standen Farm, Smarden,
Biddenden, Kent TN27 8JT
Simon Horn Furniture
117–21 Wandsworth Bridge Rd
London SW6 2TP
Liberty
Regent Street
London W1R 6AH
Lunn Antiques
86 New Kings Road
London SW6 2DX
The Monogrammed Linen Shop
168 Walton Street
London SW3 2JL
Catherine Nimmo
277 Lillie Road
London SW6 7LL
Nordic Style
109 Lots Road
London SW10 0RN
Pimpernel & Partners
596 Kings Road
London SW6 2DX
Reed Creative Services
151a Sydney Street
London SW3 6NT
The Source
26-40 Kensington High St
London W8 4PF
◰ Tobias & the Angel
68 White Hart Lane
London SW13 0PZ
◰ The White Company
298-300 Munster Road
London SW6 6BH

* denotes trade only. Contact the
address given for your local supplier

◰ mail order available

107

credits

Front cover picture: fabric from Cath Kidston, headboard made by Cover Up Designs of Kingsclere, pillowcase and pink blanket from Designers Guild

page 1 antique quilt from Nicole Fabre, ticking from Malabar Cotton Company
page 2 bedhangings from John Lewis, bed and sheets from Shaker
page 4 from left to right: fabrics from Osborne & Little; fabric from Sanderson, stripes from F. R. Street; plain fabric from Malabar Cotton Company, checked fabric from Designers Guild
page 5 from left to right: plain fabrics from Osborne & Little, striped fabric from Malabar Cotton Company; checked fabric from Ian Mankin, plain valance fabric from Osborne & Little; fabric from Designers Guild, trimming from V. V. Rouleaux, blanket from Ralph Lauren Home
page 6 sheet from Ralph Lauren Home
page 7 voile fabric from Osborne & Little, lining fabric from Designers Guild

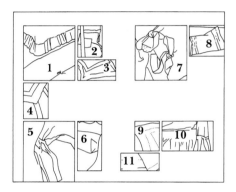

pillows and sheets pages 8–9
1 antique textiles from Tobias & the Angel
2 sheets from Shaker
3 pillowcases from Designers Guild
4 bed linen from Harrods
5 fabric from Designers Guild
6 antique bolster from Pimpernel & Partners
7 pillowcase by Damask
8 pillow from Pierre Frey
9, 10, 11 assortment of antique linens from Lunn Antiques

projects: *buttoned bolster:* fabric from Designers Guild • *trimmed ticking:* fabric from Malabar Cotton Company, trimming from John Lewis • *piqué pillows with bows:* both fabrics from McCulloch & Wallis • *velvet-edged pillowcase:* fabric from Ian Mankin, velvet trimming from V. V. Rouleaux, antique linen sheet from Tobias & the Angel • *red-trimmed linen:* fabric from Designers Guild, trimming from V. V. Rouleaux

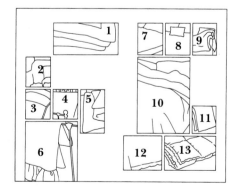

bedspreads pages 30–31
1 fabric from Shaker
2 crocheted bedspread from Liberty
3 quilt from The Conran Shop
4 blanket from Tobias & the Angel, fabric from McKinney & Co
5 fabric from Ian Mankin, quilted by Eiderdown Studio
6 sheet from Ralph Lauren Home
7 antique quilt from Nicole Fabre, ticking from Malabar Cotton Company
8 bedspread from Lunn Antiques
9 quilt from Damask
10 antique bedspread from Pimpernel & Partners
11 wool blanket from The Cross
12 lace bedspread from Liberty
13 antique eiderdown from Tobias & the Angel

projects: *appliquéd quilted bedspread:* fabric from Sanderson, striped cotton from F. R. Street • *featherstitched patchwork quilt:* made by Tobias & the Angel • *stencilled duvet cover:* fabric from Malabar Cotton Company • *velvet-edged bedspread:* fabric from F. R. Street, velvet piping from V. V. Rouleaux

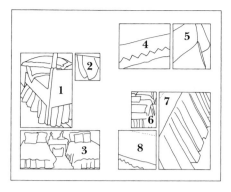

valances pages 48–49
1 & 2   organza from McCulloch & Wallis, pillowcases from The Conran Shop
3   blankets from The Conran Shop, valance fabric and pillows from Housemade,
4   quilt from Tobias & the Angel, lace edging from Lunn Antiques, checked fabric from The Blue Door
5   fabric from Manuel Canovas
6 & 7   fabric from Housemade
8   antique quilts and linens from Lunn Antiques

projects: *tailored pictorial print:* fabric from Christopher Moore Textiles • *soft green scallops:* fabric from Osborne & Little • *appliquéd zigzags:* plain fabric from Malabar Cotton Company, checked fabric from Designers Guild

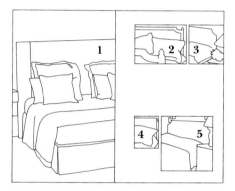

headboards pages 62–63
1   interior design by Reed Creative Services, all fabrics through Reed Creative Services
2   headboard from Simon Horn Furniture
3   headboard fabric from Colefax & Fowler
4   headboard fabric from F. R. Street
5   headboard fabric from Christopher Moore Textiles

projects: *florals and checks:* fabric from Cath Kidston, headboard made by Cover Up Designs of Kingsclere, pillowcase and pink blanket from Designers Guild • *tie-on padding:* fabric from Designers Guild • *hanging panels:* plain fabrics from Osborne & Little, striped fabric from Malabar Cotton Company • *daisy motif headboard:* fabric from KA International, red upholstery nails from The Easy Chair, headboard made by Cover Up Designs of Kingsclere

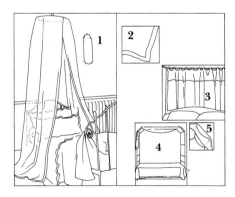

canopies pages 80–81
1 & 2   canopy from The Conran Shop, velvet ribbon from V. V. Rouleaux, sheets from The Monogrammed Linen Shop
3   fabrics from John Lewis, bed and pillowcases from Shaker
4 & 5   fabric from Liberty, bed from Designers Guild

projects: *scalloped corona:* checked fabric from Ian Mankin, valance fabric from Osborne & Little, corona from The Blue Door • *voile bed canopy:* voile from Osborne & Little, lining from Designers Guild • *tie-on bed curtains:* fabric from Shaker • *striped canopy:* fabrics from Osborne & Little

page 98   antique textiles from Tobias & the Angel
page 106   antique quilt from Nicole Fabre, ticking from Malabar Cotton Company
page 110   valance fabric and pillows from Housemade, blankets from The Conran Shop
page 111   antique eiderdown from Tobias & the Angel
page 112   blanket from Tobias & the Angel, checked fabric from McKinney & Co
endpapers: antique bolster from Pimpernel & Partners

glossary

Appliqué
Applying a second layer of fabric to a main fabric, usually with decorative stitching.

Bias binding
A strip of cloth cut on the bias, at 45° to the selvedge, which gives stretch to the fabric. Used as edging or to cover piping cord.

Bolster
A long cylindrical pillow or cushion with flat ends.

Box pleat
A flat symmetrical pleat formed by folding the fabric to the back at each side of the pleat.

Braid
A woven ribbon used as edging or trimming.

Corona
A circular or semi-circular structure fixed to the wall above a bed or sofa which has draperies suspended from it.

Flange
A flat rim or border running around a pillow or cushion.

Gingham
A plain weave cotton cloth with a checked pattern.

Inverted pleat
A tailored pleat formed like a box pleat in reverse, so the edges of the pleat meet and conceal the additional fabric.

Linen
A strong and flexible fabric spun from the fibres of the flax plant. Creases easily so is often combined with another fibre, such as cotton.

Lining fabric
A secondary fabric used to back curtains, valances and bed-spreads to protect them from light and dust. Usually a cotton sateen fabric with a slight sheen.

Matelasse
A thick double cotton cloth, stitched at regular intervals to create a luxurious quilted effect.

Mitre
The neat diagonal join of two pieces of fabric where they meet at a corner.

Organza
A stiff, thin, sheer fabric.

Piping
A length of cord covered with bias binding and used as a decorative edging.

Piqué
A type of weave that produces a hard-wearing cloth with a ribbed texture and crisp finish.

Pleat
A fold or crease, pressed or stitched in place.

Raw edge
The cut edge of fabric, without selvedge or hem.

Seam allowance
The narrow strip of raw-edged fabric left to either side of a stitched seam.

Selvedge
The defined warp edge of the fabric, specially woven to prevent unravelling.

Sheers
Fine, translucent fabrics such as muslin, voile or net that filter daylight and sunshine while preserving privacy.

Silk
A luxurious and soft yet strong fabric produced from a fibre spun by silkworms.

Stencil
A thin sheet of card or metal pierced with a simple pattern which is then brushed over with paint, leaving the pattern on the surface beneath the stencil.

Template
A shape cut from card or paper and used to mark specific outlines on fabric.

Ticking
A striped, closely woven heavy cotton twill fabric, usually with a fine stripe.

Toile de Jouy
A cotton cloth printed with pastoral scenes in a single colour on a neutral background.

Valance
A strip of fabric that runs around the base of a bed or across the top of a window.

Velcro
A double tape used for closing. One piece of tape is covered with a synthetic fuzz while the other is covered with tiny nylon fibre hooks. When pressed together, the two fabrics cling together until they are torn apart.

Velvet
A plush, luxurious warp-pile fabric with a short, closely woven pile. Can be made from cotton or synthetic fibres.

Voile
A light plain weave cotton or man-made fabric. Suitable for sheer curtains and bed drapes.

Wadding
A thick soft padding material, made either from cotton or synthetic fibres, and used for upholstery and quilting.

Warp
The threads woven across the length of fabric.

Weft
The threads woven across the width of fabric.

Width
The distance from selvedge to selvedge on any piece of fabric.

index

acknowledgements

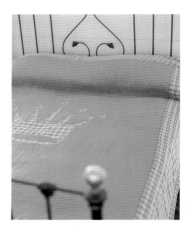

I owe a very big thank you to all the kind people who so generously gave and loaned us fabric, beds and bedding. These include The Blue Door, Jane Churchill-Wish, Designers Guild, Pierre Frey, Cath Kidston, Liberty, Malabar Cotton Co., Ian Mankin, Catherine Nimmo, Osborne & Little, V. V. Rouleaux, Arthur Sanderson and Shaker.

Many thanks to Tim Leese and Bobby Chance, Jonathan Reed, Liz Shirley, Susie Tinsley and Fiona Wheeler, all of whom kindly let us take photographs in their homes – a very disruptive activity! This book would not exist without Hänsi Schneider's exquisite sewing skills and dedication – her work continues to be inspirational. To Helena Lynch – who also made many items for photography, often in haste but always perfect – thank you.

James Merrell's photographs and complete understanding of the subject are the essence of professionalism. Lizzie Sander's illustrations are works of art that bring the sewing projects to life. They are both greatly appreciated.

The Ryland Peters & Small team continue to produce books of the highest calibre – congratulations.

Finally, to Janey Joicey-Cecil and Catherine Coombes, who have done so much of the hard work, both on photo shoots and at home, thank you both for your help.

dedication

For Carol and Mark Glasser, with everlasting friendship and love.